THE WHICH?
PLANNING AND C

THE WHICH? GUIDE TO PLANNING AND CONSERVATION

JOHN WILLMAN

Published by Consumers' Association
and Hodder & Stoughton

Which? Books are commissioned and researched by
The Association for Consumer Research
and published by Consumers' Association
2 Marylebone Road, London NW1 4DX, and
Hodder & Stoughton, 47 Bedford Square,
London WC1B 3DP

Typographic design by Paul Saunders
Cover artwork by John Holder

First edition 1990

Copyright © 1990 Consumers' Association Ltd

British Library Cataloguing in Publication Data

The Which? guide to planning and conservation.
  1. Great Britain. Planning permission
  I. Willman, John   II. Consumers' Association
  711.1

ISBN 0 340 52794 3

Typeset by Rowland Phototypesetting Ltd
Bury St Edmunds, Suffolk
Printed and bound in Great Britain by
BPCC Hazell Books
Aylesbury, Bucks
Member of BPCC Ltd

CONTENTS

ACKNOWLEDGEMENTS

This is an unusual book, in the range of subjects it covers and the variety of problems it seeks to remedy. It could not have been written without the help and advice of many people who have great knowledge and practical experience. They include Deborah Allison, John Barnes, John Barrick, Chris Brough, Tony Burton, Sue Copp, Edward Dawson, Saskia Hallam, Mark Lintel, Hilaire McCoubrey, Richard Phillips, Peter Robshaw, Avril Rodway and Philip Watts. The press officers of several government departments and many voluntary bodies and pressure groups have met my insatiable demands for material and examples with unfailing courtesy. The support of the research and editorial staff at *Which?* has been invaluable.

Margaret, Michael, Kate and Claire will all rejoice in the completion of 'that planning book'. But the real heroes of this tale are the unseen army of people who work through planning and conservation to protect and enhance our environment. They are sometimes unsuccessful in achieving their aims; their motives are often condemned; the work is always hard and unremitting. Some of their successes are used to illustrate the factual content which follows, and it is to them that this book is dedicated.

INTRODUCTION

Britain's planning system originated in the last century, with the explosive growth in towns and cities which followed the Industrial Revolution. The UK's population doubled in 50 years, and poor housing and sanitation became a danger to public health. Victorian reformers like Edwin Chadwick and Charles Kingsley campaigned for government action, and a series of *ad hoc* measures was passed giving new powers to local councils. Indeed, it was the weight of such legislation that led to a comprehensive system of local government: when it became clear that town councils and boards of health were often ill-equipped for their new tasks, first county councils and then rural and urban district councils were set up. By the beginning of the twentieth century, Britain's local government system was in place with wide powers to deal with both housing and public health.

Once basic living conditions were under control, concern soon widened to cover the environmental considerations that are at the heart of modern planning laws. For without some form of systematic planning control, economic growth produces factories cheek by jowl with housing, buildings sprawled along main roads between towns, beauty-spots ruined by quarries or factories, and sporadic development in the countryside. Piecemeal legislation tackled many of these problems in pre-war years, but the modern planning system was largely put in place by the Town and Country Planning Act of 1947.

The Act made local authorities responsible for the control of development in their areas. No development is allowed without planning permission – and for all but minor works, this requires application to the local planning authority. Central government has an important role in deciding national planning policy, co-ordinating local planning between areas and as final court of appeal for planning applications.

Since 1947 there have been many changes to the planning system, including the creation of new towns, National Parks, Areas of Outstanding Natural Beauty and conservation areas. And the planning system has been opened up to encourage participation by the public. These changes were consolidated into the Town and Country Planning Act 1971 – the law which is now in force in England and Wales. In the 1980s new ideas, such as urban development areas and enterprise zones, have been introduced to help in economic and urban regeneration. But the 1947 framework is largely intact – though creaking somewhat under the pressures of continuing rapid change.

An Englishman's home . . .

At the heart of the British planning system is the control of development. This encompasses major projects, such as an industrial estate, a shopping precinct or a housing estate. It includes making changes to your own home, whether it be adding an extension, building a new garage, putting up a satellite dish or laying a hard-standing area in front of your house. And it also covers changes in the use of buildings, from factory to warehouse, from shop to office or even converting part of your home to use for your business. No longer is the Englishman's home his castle (if, indeed, it ever were).

So with almost any significant change you might wish to make to the external appearance or use of your home, you must consider whether you need to apply for planning permission – as explained in Chapter 1. In many cases a formal application for planning permission isn't needed: common types of minor development, such as building a small extension, adding a porch or putting up a garage, are granted blanket permission – provided strict conditions are met (see Chapter 2). But if your development isn't covered by blanket permission, or if you live in a listed building or a home in certain more protected areas (see Chapter 5), you will need to apply for planning permission.

Applying for planning permission isn't something to be dreaded, however. Reasonable plans for development, in character with a home and its neighbourhood, should be allowed. In many cases the application will be made on your behalf by your builder or architect, involving little or no effort on your part. But even if this is the case, there's plenty you can do to make sure that your application goes through smoothly. The process is explained in Chapter 3, and how to appeal if your application isn't successful in Chapter 4.

Dramatis personae

Throughout this book, two key players will be your *local planning authority* and the *Secretary of State*.

The phrase 'local planning authority' is used (rather than, say, the 'council') because the relevant planning authority depends on where you live – and it may not be the local council. Since your local planning authority is the body that you will have to engage with, it is important at the outset to identify who it is.

In general, your local planning authority for getting planning permission (or opposing someone else getting it) is your district council. In London the district council is known as the London borough; in the former metropolitan counties of Greater Manchester, Merseyside, South Yorkshire, Tyne & Wear, West Midlands and West Yorkshire, it is the metropolitan district council. There are some exceptions to this general rule, which are noted where relevant (for example, if you live in a National Park, urban development area or enterprise zone).

In some areas there will be other planning bodies to deal with – county councils in the shire counties, for example, or regional councils in Scotland. In general these higher tier bodies have strategic planning functions, such as deciding on whether a whole area is residential or industrial and what roads are needed.

The other major character on the planning stage is the 'Secretary of State'. He issues policy statements and guidelines; if you appeal against a planning decision or are involved in a controversial planning issue, you could find yourself dealing with him (or, rather, his Civil Servants). In England he is the Secretary of State for the Environment; the Secretaries of State for Wales and Scotland act for those two countries.

Scotland

Scotland has its own planning system, though it is very similar to England's, set out in the Town and Country Planning (Scotland) Act 1972. Although the system is virtually the same, the legislation differs in small respects – not least the numbering of sections. This book indicates whenever possible significant differences in planning law and procedures where they apply to Scotland. But Scottish readers should bear in mind that details in this book about, for example, section numbers or certificates are those for England and Wales. Expect some differences but, unless indicated, nothing of substance.

For details of useful sources of information on the Scottish system, see p. 203.

Northern Ireland

Planning in Northern Ireland is controlled by the Planning (Northern Ireland) Order 1972, as amended in 1982. The planning authority is the Department of the Environment: although local councils are consulted on planning applications, they have no powers to decide them. Similarly, the Department is responsible for drawing up a regional plan for the province and for local plans (local authorities are consulted on this too).

Applying for planning permission in Northern Ireland is much the same as in the rest of the United Kingdom. But there is a major difference when it comes to appeals, since the Secretary of State for the Environment cannot act as appeals court on the decisions of his own Department. There is a special independent Planning Appeals Commission which can call in applications, hear appeals and preside at inquiries, as do the inspectors in England and Wales. The commissioners are appointed by the Secretary of State for Northern Ireland.

For more information about Northern Ireland, get *Your Home and Planning Permission* from the Department of the Environment for Northern Ireland (see p. 195 for address).

Improving your area

The planning system isn't just there for when you want to alter your home; it can help you to conserve and enhance the quality of your neighbourhood. There are also many other powers vested in local authorities to clean up the immediate environment in the widest sense. The second section of this book describes how to harness these laws to improve your surroundings.

Chapter 6 describes the rights you have as a householder to help protect your home against neighbours' actions which would worsen your quality of life. While resorting to the law is not a recipe for good relations with your neighbours, it may be the only redress in some circumstances.

Chapter 7 looks at what you can do if your neighbour puts in a planning application that you're not happy about. It explains how to object to a planning application and gives tips on presenting your objection in the best possible way. If your neighbour is denied planning permission, he or she can appeal against the decision – the chapter explains how you can continue your objection at the appeal.

Finally, Chapter 8 delves into ways of using the planning system and other laws to improve your area, whether it be tidying up dereliction, cutting down on noisy traffic or improving amenities. Working with others locally should improve your chances of success – the book shows how you can form a local amenity group and campaign successfully to protect and improve your environment.

New challenges

The planning stories which hit the headlines, however, are those relating to major development projects. And these appear to be getting bigger, affecting the lives of thousands and tens of thousands of people. This reflects the major economic and social changes which Britain is experiencing (in common with most advanced industrialised countries) – changes that create pressure on the planning system:

- developers seeking sites for new towns or villages to meet the growing demand for homes outside inner-city areas threaten the Green Belt and the countryside beyond
- urban redevelopment following the decline of old heavy industries involves huge tracts of land, such as former docklands areas
- pressure on housing in rural areas prices local people out of the housing market, while increased leisure puts pressure on the very fabric of the countryside
- 'green field' industrial and shopping developments have important employment, environmental and transport consequences
- new roads and rail links may lift congestion for some while blighting the homes of others.

The last great period of redevelopment in Britain came in the post-war regeneration of towns and cities, when people were glad to be rehoused and see wartime dereliction swept away. Now, as Britain enters the last decade of the twentieth century, the atmosphere is very different. Planning, the control of the environment, is itself a major concern in a more prosperous society. Issues of planning look set to be at the centre of national debate for some time to come.

And so the third and last section of this book is devoted to explaining how you can participate in the planning system to protect your area and conserve the environment. Chapter 9 explains how local planning authorities draw up plans for their areas, and how you can influence them. There is considerable scope for participation in shaping development plans, and if you are successful in embedding your priorities in the plans for your area, you may be able to avoid undesirable developments.

If you do become involved in one of the mega-development proposals, Chapter 10 tells you how you can use the planning system to defend your area. Some recent major planning battles are described to show what works (and also what doesn't). And the appeals system, right up to the High Court and beyond, is explained.

The common weal

There's no guarantee of success in planning issues: you may not get permission for an extra room for your house, but a developer may get permission to build a new town in the countryside. It is unusual for any proposal for new development not to produce winners and losers. Few want development in their back yard, but most development has to be in someone's back yard: the hard question to face up to is, 'Whose back yard?'

And that is the strength of the planning system, for all its warts. A society where no planning controls existed would certainly be an unattractive place to live – as can often be seen on trips to countries with a less sophisticated system than the UK's. But it would be equally unpleasant to live in a society where any individual could block development which affected his or her environment, regardless of the benefits to others. Planning tries to reconcile individual and collective rights: it is a publicly accountable way of deciding whose back yard is to be unlucky (or sometimes lucky).

In making these decisions, the planning system also offers an open forum to discuss major environmental issues, such as whether particular types of development are necessary.

Through the planning process, society can debate priorities for land use, evaluate the costs and benefits of projects and shape the future development of town and countryside.

Like most human endeavour, the system doesn't always succeed. But this book is designed to help you get the very best out of the planning system and to use it to improve the environment for everyone.

PART 1

Applying for Planning Permission

=== 1 ===

WHEN PLANNING PERMISSION IS NEEDED

There is a simple formula under the law to define when you need planning permission. It is that planning permission is needed whenever 'development' is to take place (with a very few exceptions). Like many such simple formulations, the reality is rather more complicated. This chapter explains what is meant by development, and the exceptions are explained in Chapter 2.

If you do have to apply for planning permission, there are several types you can apply for – details on p. 25.

Development

The official definition of 'development' in the Planning Acts is 'the carrying out of building, engineering, mining or other operations in, on, over or under land, or the making of any material change in the use of any building or land'.

For the householder this translates into three occasions on which development might take place:

- building operations – whether it be putting up a new house or adding an extension, garage, porch or whatever
- other operations – including laying a drive, putting up a radio transmitter aerial, digging a swimming-pool and erecting a fence
- change of use – splitting a house into flats, say, making it a residential nursing home or using it to sell goods.

If what you plan to do counts as development, then planning permission is necessary (unless it is one of the 'permitted developments' described in the next chapter). If you're not sure about whether you need planning permission, ask your local planning authority for a ruling (if it's not sure, ask for a Section 53 determination – see p. 26).

What happens if you ignore the planning regulations?

If you don't apply for planning permission, you may get away with it – but it's unlikely. Local planning authorities employ staff to spot people flouting the planning regulations, and neighbours often have a vested interest in making sure that transgressions do not go unpunished.

When you are rumbled, you may have to undo the work that you have done – and you could be taken to court to enforce the decision. You won't normally have to undo everything straight away (though you may have to stop what you are doing immediately – for example, using your garage as a workshop). Instead, you will be encouraged to submit an application for planning permission retrospectively. If you get the permission you needed, there will be no further comeback. But if permission is granted with conditions attached, you will have to comply with them even if the conditions involve extra expenditure.

You have the right to appeal against planning decisions, even when your application is retrospective (see Chapter 4). And you can also appeal against an enforcement notice instructing you to rectify your transgressions (see Chapter 8). But this takes you into spending a lot of time, and perhaps big money – so it's better to stick to the rules from the start.

Building Regulations

Even if you do not need planning permission for the work you intend to do, you may still need the approval of the building inspectors. Plans for new buildings, extensions and conversions must be submitted for their approval, and work may be inspected while in progress and on completion. Some small works, such as conservatories and open-sided car ports, do not require approval.

Building inspectors are employees of the local council, and their job is to make sure that you comply with the Building Regulations in any work you do. The Regulations protect you and the public at large in matters of public health and safety (so you don't leave a wall unsafe, say). The inspectors also vet any plans that involve the possible conservation of energy and are a valuable source of advice and protection for the householder.

Building operations

You need planning permission to build a new house – or any other premises, like shops or offices. Oddly, you don't at present need permission to demolish an existing building unless it is listed (see p. 90) or in a special area (p. 97).

Planning permission is needed whether the building is a new one on a 'virgin' plot, a replacement for an old building or an extra building on an existing plot. The latter is increasingly common with soaring land prices: people with large gardens in expensive city areas can make large sums of money by selling off part of their garden for a new house – so long as they can get planning permission.

But alterations to existing buildings also count as building operations, and require planning permission. Such alterations include an addition to the structure of your house, such as an extension or porch, or any other building work that materially affects the outside of the building. In practice many of the most common building alterations for private homes are covered by the permitted development exemptions described in the next chapter – though not for listed buildings or homes in special areas (see Chapter 5).

Repairs and decoration

You don't need to apply for planning permission for repairs, maintenance or decoration inside your home. You can also alter the number of rooms, move a kitchen or bathroom, or otherwise alter the internal layout (so long as you don't change their use – see opposite). These operations don't count as development (though you may need listed building consent with a listed building – see p. 90).

The same applies in general to repairs, maintenance and decoration outside the house (including re-roofing). You can paint your home any colour so long as it isn't advertising something, making an announcement or giving directions. You don't need planning permission to replace your front door or fit new windows. And you can cover your house with stone cladding or pebble dashing.

However, you may have to apply for planning permission if repairs involve adding to the structure – for example, building a higher wall at the front of your house. The same applies to decoration: adding an overhanging bay window to the front of a terraced house which had no front garden, for example, would require planning permission as an extension.

Note that work on the outside of a listed building or a home in a special area may need permission – see Chapter 5.

Other operations

Work on your home and garden which is not strictly building also requires planning permission unless it is one of the types of permitted development described in Chapter 2.

Thus, digging out a swimming-pool or artificial lake might require permission, and so might putting up walls, fences and gates, or laying down a hard standing area for your car. Erecting a radio transmitting aerial or attaching a satellite dish to your home counts as a building operation. And digging out a septic tank or cesspool also counts as development.

Change of use

Any 'material' change of use requires planning permission. To help decide when changes of use occur, the Secretary of State specifies various different classes, such as shops, offices, factories, warehouses and so on. If a building is to change from one use class to another, planning permission is normally required. If it changes its purpose but the new purpose is in the same class as the old one, then there is taken to be no change of use.

For example, converting a factory into a shop involves changing the use class, and is development. Changing from a hairdresser's to a grocer's is not development, because both are within the same class. Bank and building society branches aren't in the same class as shops, so planning permission is needed to convert one to the other. But offices and light industrial use are grouped together, and permission isn't needed to switch between them (light industries are defined as those that could reasonably be carried on in a residential area).

You can use your house for any purpose incidental to living in it without involving development. So you can keep your touring caravan in the garden or service your car in the garage without planning permission. But you must apply for planning permission when the use is more than incidental to living in the house – if you start mending other people's cars in your garage other than on a casual basis, say.

Working from home

Working from home may need planning permission if it involves a 'material' change in the use. This depends on the circumstances: writing poetry or novels in your study is unlikely to count as a material change, nor are handicrafts on a small scale. And even larger scale activity may not require planning permission, depending on the nature of the work.

But any of the following could contribute to material changes:

- using more than one room for the business activity
- using more than one machine (or set of machinery)
- employing people to work in your home
- making a lot of noise or disturbance for neighbours
- attracting numbers of callers
- displaying external advertising signs
- receiving and despatching deliveries.

Broadly, if no one is likely to notice that you are working from home, you are unlikely to need planning permission. If in doubt, speak to your local planning authority for guidance. In England and Wales ask for the free booklet *A Step-by-Step Guide to Planning Permission for Small Businesses*, prepared by the Department of the Environment.

If planning permission is needed, it may be granted only if certain conditions are met to reduce noise and disturbance. For example, there could be limits on working hours, restrictions on the number of machines, or requirements to reduce smells or noise. The local planning authority can stop you working from home if planning permission is refused.

Lodgers and sub-letting

Taking in a lodger or two is unlikely to need planning permission, so long as they are living with you as members of the family. If you move any way towards creating a separate housing unit – a bedsit or flatlets, for example – then planning permission will definitely be needed. You will also need planning permission to set up a bed-and-breakfast business or a guest-house, because this will attract more callers and possibly create disturbance to neighbours.

When you apply for planning permission to divide a house or create a guest-house, the local planning authority will consider arrangements for parking and whether your proposal would materially affect the area as it is planned to be. They may also reject a proposal to divide a house into flats if it results in the loss of accommodation suitable for a single family.

Special cases

The rules above describe the planning laws applying to buildings. But there are special laws for two other cases:

- trees
- outdoor advertisements.

Trees

Chopping down trees does not count as 'development' under the planning laws (though it may need permission from the Forestry Commission). But trees are covered by the planning legislation and can be protected under it by means of a Tree Preservation Order (TPO). And if you want to do something to a tree in a conservation area, you must give the local planning authority six weeks' notice so that it can decide if it wants to put a Tree Preservation Order on it first (see p. 96).

A Tree Preservation Order is made by the local planning authority, and can apply to a single tree, a group of trees or woodland as a whole. Hedgerows are not covered, although trees in a hedgerow can be.

You cannot fell a tree covered by a Tree Preservation Order without the consent of the local planning authority. Nor can you lop or pollard it without permission (lopping is chopping off branches with anything bigger than secateurs). You must also avoid:

- uprooting such a tree – by adjacent building work, for example
- wilfully damaging it – by hooliganism, say
- wilfully destroying one – whether by negligence (for example, damaging the roots while working nearby) or by intention (poisoning it, say).

The only exception to these extensive protective restrictions applies to a tree which is dangerous, dying or dead. You can fell a tree covered by an Order which is leaning dangerously after a gale (although you might have to replace it with a similar tree). Where woodland is covered, normal forestry operations may be allowed by the Tree Preservation Order so long as replacement trees are planted.

There are heavy fines for breaking the terms of a Tree Preservation Order. You may also have to plant a replacement of appropriate size and species.

Outdoor advertisements

Special complicated planning regulations apply to outdoor advertising, whether new or existing. The regulations cover any 'word, letter, model, sign, placard, board, notice, device or representation, whether illuminated or not, in the nature of . . . advertisement, announcement or direction'.

Some advertisements are outside the planning system altogether, including (within limits):

- advertisements on private land which are not visible from outside the land – for example in a sports stadium
- advertisements inside a building, so long as they are not illuminated or within a metre of a window
- advertisements on vehicles
- advertisements which are part of the structure of the building, such as the famous oxo building on the South Bank of the Thames
- advertisements on things for sale or vending machines, so long as they are less than 0.1 square metres in area.

Some official bodies like local councils and electricity boards are given blanket consent for official notices, etc. So too are certain signs and posters you might put up at your home, school, church or village hall (see p. 41). Travelling circuses and fairs have limited rights to put up temporary notices. And you can put a sign on business premises advertising the business (within limits).

For the rest, permission is needed from the local planning authority. And you may need permission even for some of the exceptions listed above in an Area of Special Control of

Advertisements or certain other special areas. For more about the rules covering advertising and planning, and the limits that apply when permission isn't needed, get advice from your local planning authority. There's a useful booklet outlining the rules for England and Wales, *Outdoor advertisements and signs: a guide for advertisers*, which should be available from your local planning authority.

Types of planning permission

In most cases you will be applying for full planning permission, giving complete details of your plans. If the local planning authority gives you the go-ahead, it will be unconditional or subject to certain clearly defined conditions which you must observe. But provided you stick to your plans and meet any conditions imposed in giving permission, there is no further need to involve the planning authorities.

However, there is a half-way house to allow you to see if a type of development is possible without submitting detailed plans. This is outline planning permission. And if you want to know whether planning permission is necessary at all, you can apply for a ruling known as a Section 53 determination.

Outline planning permission

If you want to sound out the local planning authority on what the likely response is to a planning application to build a property, you can apply for outline planning permission. You might wish to do this, for example, to avoid incurring the expense of a detailed plan if it will be ruled out of court. And you would normally seek outline planning permission where you are selling land for development, like a spare patch of garden: the buyer needs some indication that the development is possible if he or she is not to buy a pig in a poke. Note that you can't apply for outline planning permission for a change of use or alterations and extensions.

25

With an application for outline planning permission, you don't have to put in detailed plans. You can simply apply for outline permission for, say, a four-bedroom, two-storey detached house with two-car garage (specifying the overall area and volume, perhaps). You can put in a rudimentary layout with details to be filled in later, or even simple plans with the proviso that they may be substantially revised. In some circumstances the local planning authority will consider outline planning permission applications only if fairly detailed plans are drawn up – still allowing some leeway for revision later. And where the details are very important in a planning decision (listed buildings, say, or a conservation area), the local planning authority can decline an outline application altogether.

If outline planning permission is granted, no work can begin until all the details have been approved. You seek this by a further application to approve 'reserved matters', submitting all the missing details. If this is not done, after a period of time – normally three years – the outline planning permission will lapse unless you apply to renew it.

Section 53 determination

Under Section 53 of the Town and Country Planning Act 1971, you can ask the local planning authority to rule on whether some development you intend to carry out needs planning permission or not. If you are in any doubt, this is the only way to get an authoritative ruling: once you have been given the go-ahead, you cannot be made to undo the work later. To get a ruling, simply write to the local planning authority giving a full description of your plans and asking whether they count as 'development' and, if so, whether planning permission is required.

You can't ask for a Section 53 determination for work that has already started. And the answer may be that a planning application is needed – in which case you are no worse off than before.

How planning decisions are made

For all but the most exceptional planning cases, your application for planning permission will be decided by the local planning authority. Once it gives you permission, unconditionally or with conditions which are acceptable to you, you can go ahead; no one can then appeal against the decision (except on technical legal reasons). But if you are refused permission, or unacceptable conditions are imposed, you can appeal against the local planning authority's decision to the Secretary of State.

In cases which are controversial or of national importance, the Secretary of State can call in the planning application to decide it for himself. This will be at a public inquiry, and the Secretary of State's decision cannot be appealed against (again, except on technical legal reasons).

The Flowchart on p. 29 illustrates the planning process you will have to go through.

How planning applications are decided

The central principle for planning decisions is that people should be free to develop their homes and land as they wish unless there is a good reason why they shouldn't. You do not have to provide a positive justification for your application, and the planning authority does not have to give a reason for approving it. But it does have to have a good planning reason for rejecting it.

For example, there are practical considerations, such as the proposed design, the appearance of the result and how it fits in with its surroundings. The development may impinge on the surrounding transport arrangements and have implications for services such as water and sewerage.

There are also strategic implications to consider: is there too much of this sort of development in the area already; will more of this type change the character of the area; will it remove other more valuable amenities from the area; will it damage the countryside?

27

TIP

Don't rely on the word of a salesman who says that you don't need planning permission for a loft extension kit, prefabricated garage or conservatory. Many salesmen have no training in planning law, and no two planning cases are the same. Even if the salesman puts it in writing, you're no better off – he hasn't the power to grant planning permission. And unless you employed the salesman as a planning specialist, you can't sue for compensation.

The criteria that apply to any particular case depend on the case itself, and thus different weight will be assigned to the criteria according to their relevance. Indeed, if you end up challenging a planning decision, you can argue that not only is a factor irrelevant on planning grounds, but also that the factor is not relevant in that particular case.

Overall, the most important yardstick in making the planning decision should be the development plan which local planning authorities draw up for your area (see p. 159). A proposal that fits in with the policies of the plan is less likely to be refused than one that doesn't – even if there are other aspects of it which are less attractive.

If the decision is to turn down your application, the local planning authority must give the reasons for its decision.

Getting professional advice

As noted earlier, a builder or architect working for you will normally deal with planning as part of the job. If you are not using such people (or your builder doesn't deal with planning matters), you can use the services of a planning consultant to help you with your application.

A town planning consultant is the professional in this field. Look for a Member or Fellow of the Royal Town Planning

THE PLANNING PROCESS

1. You submit a planning application to the local planning authority.

2. The Secretary of State for the Environment can call it in to decide himself (controversial cases only) after a public inquiry. If he does, GO TO 6.

3. The local planning authority considers the application. Three possible outcomes:
    (i) Permission granted. GO AHEAD.
    (ii) Permission granted with conditions. GO TO 4.
    (iii) Permission refused. GO TO 5.

4. Are the conditions acceptable?
    YES. GO AHEAD.
    NO. GO TO 5.

5. Do you want to appeal?
    YES. GO TO 6.
    NO. PROPOSAL IS LOST (you could amend and resubmit).

6. Written appeal, informal hearing or public inquiry to decide the issue. Three possible outcomes:
    (i) Appeal upheld. GO AHEAD.
    (ii) Appeal upheld with conditions. GO AHEAD IF ACCEPTABLE; IF NOT, GO TO 7.
    (iii) Appeal rejected. GO TO 7.

7. Can process be challenged in the High Court?
    IF YES, CONSIDER A CHALLENGE.
    IF NOT, PROPOSAL IS LOST (you could amend and resubmit).

Institute (MRTPI or FRTPI). Anyone who describes him- or herself as a 'chartered town planner' must also be a Member or Fellow of the RTPI. The Royal Town Planning Institute can supply a list for your area (see p. 198 for the address), or look in Yellow Pages under Town Planning Consultants. A local firm of architects may also be prepared to work for you, and some firms of solicitors have partners who are legal members of the RTPI and can advise on planning law.

Professional advice can be expensive – expect to pay at least £30 an hour for their time. If this is beyond your means, there are various voluntary planning aid groups that may be able to give advice. Ask at your local Citizens Advice Bureau or contact the Royal Town Planning Institute for details of groups in your area.

2

WHEN PLANNING
PERMISSION ISN'T NEEDED

The planning system is designed to control even quite small developments, such as house extensions and high garden walls. These can be just as intrusive as much larger works, and have the potential to make life unpleasant for neighbours. But if householders had to seek permission for every alteration to their property, the result would be a bureaucratic nightmare. So the government grants blanket planning permission for certain minor and routine types of development under a General Development Order (GDO). This means that you don't need to apply for planning permission for any of the classes of development laid down in the GDO (the most recent for England and Wales, published in 1988, has 28 such classes).

Only a few of the classes of development covered by the GDO are relevant to the ordinary householder – and they are hedged in by strict conditions and limits which must be stuck to. The rules apply to houses only: if you live in a flat or maisonette, ask your local planning authority whether permission is needed. And if your development doesn't meet the conditions about size, etc., planning permission will be needed.

Even if your development would normally be covered by the GDO, you still have to apply for planning permission if either of the following applies:

- it might create a safety hazard by obstructing the view on a road used by vehicles
- you are creating a new way on to a trunk or classified road (for people or vehicles) or enlarging an existing one.

31

And you may need planning permission even for developments permitted under the GDO if they go against the terms of the original planning permission for your house (see p. 39 for how this applies to hedges). Check with your local planning authority if you think this might apply.

TIP

Even if you don't need planning permission, you may need approval under the Building Regulations for work that you intend to do (see p. 18). Check with the building inspectors before you start work.

Remember that you can be made to undo changes you make if it turns out that you should have applied for planning permission (see p. 18). In many cases a call or visit to your local planning offices will be all that's needed to clarify the rules (confirm the advice or information by letter to put it on the record, mentioning the name of the person you spoke to and the date). If there's still some doubt about whether planning permission is required after that, ask for a Section 53 determination to get a firm ruling (see p. 26 for details).

Living in – or near – a listed building, or in a special area?

You may need planning permission to make alterations to a listed building which would not need an application for an ordinary house. This includes alterations to the interior and redecorating its exterior. There are also much stricter rules about development in conservation areas, National Parks, Areas of Outstanding Natural Beauty and certain other areas. If you think that you might be affected by these special rules, turn to Chapter 5 for more details.

Note that even if you do not live in a listed building, you may still be affected by the listed building rules if your home is within the 'curtilage' of a listed building. Curtilage is an archaic term which comes from the French word for court-yard: it would include land traditionally associated with the house, former outbuildings and other homes in the same terrace. So a house attached to or beside a listed building might fall within its curtilage.

Extensions

Planning permission is not needed for many extensions to your home, provided certain strict conditions are met.

The first is that the extension must not create a new home: this is normally taken to be a completely self-contained unit with its own bathroom, kitchen, etc. and independent access.

TIP

If you're extending your property to make a granny flat or otherwise divide the home, avoid creating a new home if you don't want to apply for planning permission. There are no hard and fast rules about when a home is created: a house shared by two families with separate facilities have been known to count as a single home. But building separate entrances will almost certainly count as creating a new home.

Increase in volume

The second set of restrictions involved in extensions limits the amount of extra space you can add without applying for planning permission. You have to apply for planning permission to build an extension which would increase the volume of your home by more than a certain amount over its 'original volume'. For a house built since 1 July 1948, the 'original volume' is its volume when built; for an older house, the 'original volume' is its volume on 1 July 1948.

In calculating the volume of your home after adding the

33

extension, you must include the following: all extensions added since the 'original volume' was calculated; outbuildings of more than ten cubic metres which are within five metres of the house; and outbuildings, however small, which will be within five metres of the house as extended. You will need to apply for planning permission if:

- for a terraced house, the new extension would take the property's volume more than 50 cubic metres over its 'original volume', or 10 per cent if this is more
- for any other sort of house, the new extension would take its volume more than 70 cubic metres (50 cubic metres in Scotland) over its 'original volume', or 15 per cent (20 per cent in Scotland) if this is more.

Whichever sort of property it is, the total increase in size over the 'original volume' cannot exceed 115 cubic metres unless you apply for planning permission. As a guide, a single-storey extension 7 by 3 metres is about 50 cubic metres in volume.

EXAMPLE: VICTORIAN VALUES

Jane Litton lives in a Victorian semi-detached house in London and wanted to extend the kitchen into the garden. The house's volume without the planned kitchen extension was 460 cubic metres. Her extension would have added 35 cubic metres, bringing the total volume to 495 cubic metres. To see whether she needed planning permission for the extension, Jane first calculated the 'original volume'. The house includes a 1950s conservatory of 24 cubic metres. Since this was added after 1 July 1948, Jane deducted its volume from the total of 460 cubic metres to find the 'original volume' of 436 cubic metres. The kitchen extension would therefore have taken the volume of her house 495−436=59 cubic metres over the 'original volume' of her house. Fifty-nine cubic metres is less than 15 per cent of the 'original volume', so Jane didn't need planning permission for her kitchen extension.

Other restrictions

Even if you are within the volume limits, there are certain other restrictions if you are to avoid applying for planning permission:

- the extension, added to previous extensions and outbuildings, must not eat up more than half the original garden area
- it cannot be higher than the highest point of the original roof of the building
- it should be no closer to a public road or footpath than the original building (or 20 metres if the original building is more than 20 metres from the road or footpath)
- any part of the extension within two metres of the boundary of your plot must not be more than four metres high.

In each case 'original' means as on 1 July 1948 or, if built since that date, as when it was built.

TIP

When measuring the volume and area of your property and your planned extension, be sure to take the outside measurements. The difference between the inside and outside measurements can be quite marked for a small extension.

Height measurements should be taken from the ground beside the building (if uneven, from the highest point).

Loft extensions

Outside Scotland, you don't need to apply for planning permission for a loft conversion, provided it is within the limits listed above for a normal extension *and* it meets the following conditions:

- its volume is no more than 50 cubic metres, or 40 cubic metres for a terraced house (this allowance is not an addition to that for a normal extension, but must be deducted from it)

- it doesn't stick out beyond the original roof on any slope facing a public highway – so you can't put a dormer extension on the road side of the house.

Note that a public highway includes any path or road used by pedestrians or vehicles. So you must get planning permission if you want to put in a dormer window on the side of a house facing a footpath, alleyway or access road. And in Scotland loft extensions always need planning permission.

Porches

Normally you need planning permission for an extension at the front of your property if the extension sticks out in front of the original line of the house. But outside Scotland you don't need to apply for planning permission to build a porch outside a door as long as the porch is within the following measurements:

- area of three square metres or less
- height above ground level of three square metres or less
- two metres or more away from the boundary of your plot with a highway (again, this includes paths and alleys).

Remember that all measurements must be taken on the *outside* of the porch.

Conservatories

If attached to your property or within five metres of it, these count towards the general limits for extensions (see above), as do sun lounges, enclosed verandahs or any other appendage to the living area.

If further than five metres from the house, any such building falls under the rules for outbuildings (see below).

Garages

A garage within five metres of the property counts as an extension to it, so you must apply for planning permission if building it means that you exceed the limits set out for extensions (see below).

If the garage is to be more than five metres from the house, it counts as an outbuilding (see below).

Outbuildings and other structures

Most outbuildings, such as a shed, summerhouse, chicken house, aviary or greenhouse, can be built without applying for planning permission. The structure must not be a new dwelling itself: it should be for 'a purpose incidental to the enjoyment' of the house. Where the outbuilding is for poultry, bees, pets, birds or other animals, such animals must be for the 'domestic needs or personal enjoyment' of the family – you can't use this exemption to avoid getting planning permission for a business.

The first point to determine is which set of planning rules applies to the building you want to put up, extend or alter. In some cases it may count as an extension to your house, governed by the rules set out above. If it falls under the different rules for outbuildings, then different rules apply (see below).

If the outbuilding is within five metres of any part of the house, it counts as an extension unless it is smaller than ten cubic metres in volume. If what you have in mind falls into this category, you must consider the rules for extensions (see above) in deciding whether you need to apply for planning permission.

If the outbuilding is further than five metres from the property (or is less than ten cubic metres in volume), then the rules below apply for deciding whether you need planning permission.

Planning permission for outbuildings

You don't need to apply for planning permission for an outbuilding so long as the following conditions are met:

37

- no more than half the original garden area (see p. 35) is covered by outbuildings and any extensions to the property
- the outbuilding is no closer to any highway (road or footpath) than the original walls of the house, or 20 metres if the house is more than 20 metres from the highway
- the structure will be no higher than four metres if it has a pitched (sloping) roof, three metres if a flat roof.

TIP

If your house is already extended, you may require planning permission to build a garage or shed adjoining it. You may be able to avoid the hassle of applying for planning permission by siting the garage more than five metres from the house, so that it counts as an outbuilding instead.

Pools, ponds and tennis courts

Swimming-pools, ponds, sauna cabins and tennis courts count as outbuildings for planning purposes, so long as they are for the incidental enjoyment of your home (not if you are setting up a health club or trout farm, for instance).

So you cannot build one of these structures in your front garden without planning permission unless it is more than 20 metres from the highway. And at least half the plot other than the original house must be left uncovered by the various additions and outbuildings if you are to avoid the need to apply for permission.

Aerials and other structures

You don't need planning permission to put a TV or radio aerial on your house. But there may be local rules about putting up aerials (for example, in a conservation area), or a covenant on every home on an estate may forbid prominent aerials (see p. 46).

Satellite dishes are a different matter: on a house you can put up one dish no more than 90 centimetres in diameter without permission, providing it isn't higher than the top of the house. If you want a second dish, this needs planning permission.

If the aerial is to be mounted on a mast in the garden, this is treated as an outbuilding for planning purposes. In other words, if it is more than three metres high above the ground, planning permission is needed (see p. 38). The same applies to a flagpole.

Storage tanks

Planning permission is needed if you want to put most types of storage tank in your garden or on your roof. But you don't need permission for a tank to store central heating oil provided it meets all the following conditions:

- its capacity is 3500 litres or less
- it reaches no more than three metres from the ground
- it is no closer to a public highway (including a footpath) than the original house itself, or 20 metres if the house is further than 20 metres from the road.

So you do need planning permission for a propane tank, or to store petrol, oil or other liquids in bulk.

Walls and fences

You can put up walls, fences and gates on your land without permission if the following restrictions are met:

- they are of a maximum height of one metre if facing a road used by cars or other vehicles
- they are of a maximum height of two metres elsewhere.

If you are repairing or replacing existing walls, fences and gates, you can do so to their former height if this is no more than in the rules above.

Note that there are no rules covering hedges or tree screens (apart from any estate covenants – see p. 46). But if you're planting one on an open-plan estate, check with the local planning authority that permission isn't needed under a condition imposed with the original planning permission for your house.

Patios, drives and hard standing

You can concrete over your entire garden, if you wish, without seeking planning permission (except in Scotland). Similarly, south of the border you can build a patio, drive, path or area of hard standing at the front.

But you may need to apply for planning permission if you make a new way on to a highway (road or path), whether by a drive or footpath. You don't need to apply if both the following conditions apply:

- the road is not a trunk or classified road (check with the local planning authority if you're not sure of its status)
- the path or driveway is part of some other development, such as a garage, for which you don't need to apply for planning permission.

Note that if you want to drop the kerb to make access to your property easier by car, you have to apply to the highway authority.

Cars, vans, caravans and boats

You can normally stand a car, caravan, boat or trailer on your land without permission. But some local authorities have powers to keep caravans and boats off front drives. Check with your local planning authority.

You can use your caravan or boat while it's on your land (including sleeping in it) as long as you don't make a separate dwelling out of it – for example, by connecting mains electricity. And you can't use it for business purposes without applying for change of use.

You may also need to apply for change of use if you stand a

vehicle used for trade on your property. This might apply to a taxi, minicab, ice-cream van or delivery van, especially if it's got the name of the business on it. Check with the local planning authority if you're not sure.

Trees

You can prune, pollard, lop or fell a tree (unless there is a Tree Preservation Order on it – see p. 23). If you live in a conservation area, you must give six weeks' notice to the local planning authority.

Advertisements

There are strict regulations covering advertisements on your home (see p. 24). But you don't normally need to apply for permission to put up the following:

- professional nameplates up to 0.3 square metres in area
- warning notices ('beware of the dog'), direction signs or house name signs up to 0.3 square metres in area
- notices on churches, hotels, pubs and certain other buildings up to 1.2 square metres in area
- temporary advertisements up to 0.5 square metres in area when selling or letting residential property (but check with the local planning authority, as many have extra rules covering these)
- notices of meetings, jumble sales, etc. for charitable purposes up to 0.6 square metres in area
- election posters for local, national or European elections – but take them down within 14 days of the poll closing
- official neighbourhood watch scheme signs (within limits).

Note that in some cases local authorities make local by-laws covering these advertisements. If in doubt, check.

WHEN PLANNING PERMISSION IS ALWAYS NEEDED

You will always need to apply for planning permission if any of the following is true of your development:

- You are creating a new way on to a trunk or classified road, or enlarging an existing one
- You might create a safety hazard for traffic
- You will create a new home
- You are changing the use of your home
- Your home will grow by more than 115 cubic metres over its original volume or exceed the other volume limits
- More than half the original garden will be covered by extensions and outbuildings
- Your alterations will come above the level of the original roof
- The alteration or extension will stick out from the front of your original house (or come within 20 metres of the public highway if the original house is more than 20 metres from the highway)
- Your extension will be more than four metres high within two metres of the boundary of your plot
- It is a loft extension bigger than 50 cubic metres (40 cubic metres for a terraced house), or with a dormer window overlooking a highway or in Scotland (see p. 35)
- It is a porch exceeding the limits on p. 36
- If more than five metres from the house, it is higher than three metres (four metres with a pitched roof)
- You are putting up a second satellite dish on a house.

Note 'Original' means as on 1 July 1948 or, if built since that date, as when built.
Highway includes footpaths and rights of way.

Minor changes of use

Almost all changes of use of buildings require you to apply for planning permission. These include:

- letting out rooms, although taking in lodgers who live as members of the family probably doesn't need an application (see p. 22)
- conversion to flats, although restoring flats into a house doesn't
- using part of your home for a business – running a catering business from the kitchen, storing things you intend to sell in the garage, parking trade vehicles on the drive, for example. In practice, small-scale working from home may not need planning permission (see p. 21).

Changing the use of non-residential property usually also requires planning permission. Changes within a particular class of use don't count as development, so you can change a clothes shop into a food shop without planning permission. And certain minor changes don't require an application – for example, changing a shop into a café. Again, check with the local planning authority.

TIP

If you're in any doubt about whether you need planning permission for an alteration or development, ask your local planning authority for guidance.

=== 3 ===

APPLYING FOR PLANNING PERMISSION

If you need to apply to your local planning authority for planning permission, be of good cheer: four out of five planning applications are successful – and the chances of success are even higher for ordinary householders.

If you are using an architect or planner for your proposed work, he or she will normally apply for planning permission on your behalf. Many builders will also do this, especially where they specialise in extensions, swimming-pools or whatever you are building. You will be listed as the applicant for planning permission, but your architect or builder, acting as your agent, signs the forms, deals with the local planning authority and receives any letters in connection with the development. Ask to be kept informed of progress by the agent and to be shown copies of decisions about planning permission (and Building Regulations).

Note that if you live in a listed building, or a special area such as a conservation area, National Park or Area of Outstanding Natural Beauty, extra steps may be needed: be sure to read Chapter 5 to see what these are.

Preparatory investigations

Before you get as far as filling in application forms, a visit to your local planning office is highly recommended. For a start, you can pick up the application forms and copies of any leaflets the local planning authority issues by way of guidance. In England and Wales ask for a copy of the free leaflet *Planning Permission: a Guide for Householders*, prepared by the Department of the Environment. Some councils produce leaflets on design and materials for buildings. Following such guidelines would improve your chances of getting permission.

If you have any questions or worries, an informal chat with a planning officer may clear things up. You may even find that no planning permission is needed for what you have in mind. You can also try to see the building inspectors if your plans need to take account of Building Regulations (see p. 18) – they'll be equally willing to clear up questions.

But a visit is also sensible because you can look at the local plan for your area if there is one. You can check the original planning permission for your house (if any) for conditions about further developments of it. You could also see whether there are any planning applications from neighbours that might throw up some interesting information.

Local plans

Your local planning authority may have produced a local plan, which spells out in some detail how it sees your area developing. If there is a current local plan, it will be an important factor in making the decision about your application.

Suppose, for example, that you want to build a workshop on to your home in an area of mixed-use buildings. You are more likely to be successful if the local plan sees mixed uses continuing and seeks to encourage small business expansion. If the plan aims to reduce business use of your area and make it a fully residential one, you could be wasting your time.

Local plans consist of a map of the area and statements summarising the planning policies and proposals for it. There will also be notes, diagrams, illustrations and whatever else is needed to explain the plan. These proposals can cover the classes of development which will be allowed or the types of land use that will be permitted in the area. Local planning authorities are encouraged to include measures to improve the environment and deal with traffic in their plans. For more about the planning system, see p. 159.

An application that fits into the policies of the local plan is much more likely to succeed. By studying the plan, you may find ways of presenting your proposal, or tailoring it in some ways, so as to improve its chances. The plan may get pretty detailed – for example, the number of houses per acre, the size of houses, and so on. Any such detail can help you formulate your proposal to fit with the local plan.

Any restrictive covenants?

One last piece of preparatory work is to find out whether there are any restrictive covenants applying to your house. These are often drawn up by developers to preserve the character of the estates they build, and imposed on the buyers in the contract of sale. Each buyer is required to agree to impose the same covenants on anyone they sell the house to. And when selling the house, they can add further covenants: where someone builds a new house on land beside their old one, they may impose covenants on the buyer of their old house – for example, to provide access to the new one or to protect their privacy.

Covenants can ban infilling (splitting a garden to create a second plot for housing) or dividing a house into flats. They can stop you building large outhouses or garages, hanging washing outdoors, putting up TV aerials, parking a caravan or boat on the drive, erecting hedges or fences on open-plan estates, or even repainting the outside of the house other than in certain colours. If you are bound by a covenant which forbids the development you wish to carry out, getting planning permission does not mean you can go ahead (though covenants can be overridden by planning law – for example, on allowing telephone wires to cross land).

So it's worth checking that your house isn't covered by covenants which would stop you doing the work you want to do. The solicitors who handled the house purchase should be

able to advise, and may have sent you details of any covenants at the time you bought it. Covenants can be removed
(at some cost), but they can also be enforced by neighbours or
others with an interest and should not be ignored.

Filling in the forms

The local planning authority will usually have a pack of
forms, some of which will not apply to private housing or
your application. This should include some notes about
filling in the forms and enclosures needed with your application – study these carefully before putting pen to paper.

The exact forms you will have to complete depend on the
type of application you are making and the procedures laid
down by your local planning authority. But all applicants
have to fill in a form requiring general information, often
called Form TP1, 1A or PA1. This asks for:

- the name, address and telephone number of the applicant
- the name, address and telephone number of any agent –
  the builder or architect, for example
- the address of the house or land the planning application is
  for
- brief details of the development proposed – 'double
  garage' or 'two-storey extension', for example
- the type of application – full, outline, approval of reserved
  matters (see p. 25) or whatever
- some information about the development, such as
  whether it involves change of use, new or altered access to
  a highway, felling trees, and so on
- details of the present use of the buildings or land, or, if
  vacant, their previous use.

If the planning application is for mining, industrial, office,
warehousing, storage or shops, there will be other forms to
fill in. These ask about matters such as any processing to be
carried out, machinery to be installed, parking, loading and
unloading, refuse and effluent disposal, use of dangerous

TIP

If your home is jointly owned with someone else (your
spouse, for example), put both names as applicants. This
avoids the need to fill in another form saying that all owners
have been notified (see below).

---

materials, and so on. You must also give some detailed
measurements of the floor space to be devoted to different
uses – retailing, storage, etc.

Maps, plans and drawings

Your application must be accompanied by a map which
identifies the site, and plans and drawings 'as are necessary
to describe the development'. If you are using a builder or
architect, producing these maps, plans and drawings should
be part of his or her service. If not, you will have to provide
them yourself, to a standard acceptable to your local planning
authority.

The map should be drawn in a way that enables the local
planning authority to compare it with the Ordnance Survey
maps for the area. It should be at least 1:2500 in scale (that is,
1 centimetre on the map represents 25 metres in real life); it
is usual – and essential for urban areas – to use the more
detailed 1:1250 scale (1 centimetre represents 12.5 metres).
The easiest approach is to get a copy of the Ordnance Survey
map for your road to the right scale – there's probably one
with the papers drawn up when you bought your house (ask
the solicitor who handled the purchase). You should be able
to get a copy at your local library or perhaps the council
planning office (for a fee).

Mark the boundaries of the site where the development is
to take place in red on the map. If you own any of the land
adjoining the site, outline that in blue. And check that the
map is up to date – draw in by hand any new buildings,
paths, roads, changes of use, etc.

If you are building or altering a house, you should also include a block plan with your application. This is the sort of plan drawn up by architects and draughtsmen – it used to be on blue-tinted paper – which is an accurate representation of the site as it is, with details of your proposals. It should include such items as trees, access, services such as cables and pipes, drainage and so on, drawn to a scale of 1:500.

Lastly, detailed building plans should also be included, with plans, elevations, cross-sections and enlargements of details. The scale is normally 1:100, and information about materials to be used, special operations to strengthen the building, colours of bricks and woodwork, type of flooring, etc. is usually given.

If you are competent with pen and ruler, you may be able to draw up your own plans, especially for simple alterations such as a porch. There is often a block plan attached to the documents prepared when buying a house (check with your solicitor) which is a good starting-point. Ask friends who've had similar work done for a look at their plans to get an idea of what's needed. If you're using a kit (for a conservatory, say), this may have standard plans included.

You can get the right sort of materials from an artists' supplies shop – tough paper that will survive frequent folding and unfolding, fine ink pens, and so on. But it may be easier just to do the drawings in pencil on tracing paper (available in A4, A3 and A2 sizes) and make as many photocopies as you need. Local photocopying and print shops can often make large-scale photocopies or blow up small-scale plans to working size.

With all but the simplest developments, it may involve less hassle in the long run to get a professional job done. A freelance draughtsman would be able to produce the drawings for straightforward home improvements for around £100 or less – and you'd probably get some worthwhile advice about methods into the bargain. If you need help with design or the site needs measuring up by the draughtsman, the cost could be higher. Ask friends, an estate agent or a builder for a recommendation, or try Yellow Pages.

Fees

You have to pay a fee for most planning applications, on a complex scale set down by the government. The scale is revised (normally upwards!) from time to time. The fees for the most common types of application, current in summer 1990, are set out opposite.

There is no charge for asking for a ruling that planning permission is not needed (a Section 53 determination – see p. 26). Nor is there any fee if you submit a revised application within 12 months of being refused planning permission for the same development (or within 12 months of submitting the original application if you withdrew it). Certain special consents you need in addition to planning permission are also free: listed building consent (see p. 90) and conservation area consent (see p. 97). And there is no fee for work aimed solely at improving a disabled person's access, safety, health or comfort at home.

TIP

If the correct fee is not received with your application, the application is not processed until the correct fee is sent – so your application could be delayed. Check first to whom you make the cheque payable.

Certification of Ownership

The application must be accompanied by a Certification of Ownership (known as a Section 27 Certificate), saying that the owners are aware of the application. An owner for these purposes is anyone who 21 days before the date of the application has an interest in the freehold or a lease with more than seven years left to run. If any of the land is agricultural land, any tenant counts as an owner in this context.

If the applicant is the sole owner, or the joint applicants are

---

FEES FOR PLANNING APPLICATIONS

Alterations or extensions
   1 house or flat   £38
   2 or more houses or flats   £66

New house or flats
   Outline permission   £76 per 0.1 hectare*
   Full permission   £76 per house or flat**

Other buildings
   Up to 40 square metres floor area   £38
   Over 40 and up to 75 square metres   £76
   Each further 75 square metres   £76**

Converting house to flats   £76 per flat**

Change of use   £76

Advertisement
   For business on premises   £21
   Directing people to business   £21
   Others   £76

Approval of reserved matters
   Depends – ask local planning authority

*   maximum £1900
**   maximum £3800

---

the joint owners, they or their agent simply sign a statement to that effect. This statement (sometimes called Certificate A) may be a separate form or be part of the main application form. If there is more than one owner, or the owner is not making the application, there are procedures to follow to get their agreement.

Note that similar procedures apply in Scotland, but that the Sections of the Planning Act are different (as are the exact wordings of the various certificates and notices).

If the applicant is not the sole owner

If there is an owner who is not one of the applicants, he or she must be given notice of the application. This allows him or her to inspect the plans and make representations if he or she wishes to. A certificate will have to be signed saying that this has been done.

This could be necessary in many cases:

- where a house is jointly owned by a couple but one of the partners is estranged and has moved out; the estranged partner must be notified so long as he or she remains an owner
- with a leasehold house, the freeholder remains an owner for the purposes of planning applications (as well as the leaseholder who will in all probability be the person applying for planning permission)
- where someone is going to buy a property only if planning permission is given, they will be applying even though they are not the owner.

There is a standard form of notice to be sent to owners in these cases (this should also be sent to agricultural tenants – see above). The example on p. 53 shows one of these, with the details (in *italics*) filled in – note that it has to be sent not earlier than 21 days before the application is made. Once this is done, you can sign the appropriate certification that notice has been given, either on the application form or in the package which accompanies it (often called Certificate B).

If you cannot contact any of the owners, you have to put an advertisement in a local newspaper – again, not earlier than 21 days before the date of application for planning permission. The wording of the advertisement is specified in planning law, and is identical to the form of notice shown on p. 53. A copy of this advertisement must be sent in with the application, together with either Certificate C (if you have managed to contact some of the owners) or Certificate D (where you cannot reach any of the owners).

NOTICE OF PLANNING APPLICATION TO BE SENT TO OWNERS (ENGLAND AND WALES)

Town and Country Planning Act 1971

NOTICE UNDER SECTION 27 OF APPLICATION
FOR PLANNING PERMISSION

Proposed development at *33 Acacia Avenue, Slagthorpe, Borsetshire.*

I give notice that *Michael John Smith* is applying to the *Slagthorpe District* Council for planning permission to *erect a two-storey extension.*

Any owner* of the land who wishes to make representations about this application should write to the Council at *Slagthorpe District Council Planning Department, Town Hall, Slagthorpe, Borsetshire* within 21 days of the date of service/~~publication~~** of this notice.

* 'owner' means a person having a freehold interest or a leasehold interest the unexpired term of which is not less than seven years, or, in the case of development consisting of the winning or working of minerals, a person entitled to an interest in a mineral in the land (other than oil, gas, coal, gold or silver).

Signed: *Michael John Smith*

** ~~On behalf of:~~

Date: *10 September 1990*

** Delete where inappropriate

Neighbours

You don't normally have to tell your neighbours that you have applied for planning permission, except with 'bad neighbour' developments – see below. But in Scotland you do have to notify neighbours, by serving a notice on the owners of adjoining property – details of the form of notice are available from the local planning authority.

TIP

Always inform your neighbours about planning applications – and consider consulting them in advance. Their opposition could be influential in deciding whether your application is accepted or not. Getting them on your side – or at least not getting them agitated because your application is sprung on them – is good tactics.

Even if you don't have to tell neighbours about your application, your local planning authority probably will if the proposal affects them in any way. If the local authority doesn't tell your neighbours, they may get to hear about your application in other ways: on the grapevine, for example. And with listed buildings and special areas like conservation areas, the application will be advertised in the local newspaper (see pp. 93 and 98).

If your neighbours are totally opposed to what you want to do, that shouldn't necessarily stop you putting in an application. After listening to their views, you can submit a written statement with your application dealing with what appear to be their objections. Much more likely is that your neighbours will want reassurance about your plans – that your alterations won't ruin the look of their houses, or that the work will be done without undue disruption. It makes sense to tailor your application to meet such objections (in the interests of good neighbourliness, as well as improving your chances of success).

Bad neighbour developments

In a limited number of cases you are required to inform neighbours of developments which may not be nice to live next door to. These 'bad neighbour' developments are work in connection with any of the following classes of Article 11 of the General Development Order 1988 (England and Wales):

(a) construction of buildings for public conveniences
(b) refuse or waste disposal operations (including scrap dealings and coalyards)
(c) mining
(d) sewerage (though not for single buildings where not more than ten people will normally live or work)
(e) putting up tall buildings (more than 20 metres high)
(f) slaughterhouse, knacker's yard or poultry killing or plucking
(g) entertainment such as a casino, fun-fair or bingo hall, a cinema, theatre, music hall, dance hall, skating rink, sports hall, swimming-bath or gym (unless part of a school, college or university), Turkish baths or other vapour or foam bath
(h) a zoo, or boarding or breeding cats or dogs
(i) motor car or motor cycle racing
(j) a stadium
(k) a cemetery or crematorium.

If any of these bad neighbour developments is involved, you have to advertise it in a local newspaper in the form shown on p. 56 (this is known as a Section 26(2) advertisement, after the appropriate clause of the Town and Country Planning Act 1971). A copy of this advertisement must be submitted with the planning application, together with a certificate giving the date and newspaper name.

A similar notice must be put up at the site for at least seven days (unless you can't get access to the site because you have

---

TIP

In view of these strict extra requirements – and the likelihood of opposition from other people locally – get professional advice with 'bad neighbour' developments (see p. 28).

---

no right of way). After it has been up for the seven days, a further certificate (called a Section 26(2) certificate) must be sent in confirming that the site notice has been displayed for the required time. There are separate certificates to send in if the notice is defaced or removed or if you can't get access to the site.

NOTIFICATION FOR BAD NEIGHBOUR DEVELOPMENTS (ENGLAND AND WALES)

Town and Country Planning Act 1971

NOTICE UNDER SECTION 26(2)

Proposed development at *The Larches, Ivy Lane, Borminster Newton, Borsetshire.*

I give notice that *Mary Diana Peggoty* is applying to the *Slagthorpe District* Council for planning permission to *erect a building for dog boarding kennels under Class H of Article 11 of the General Development Order 1988.*

Members of the public may inspect copies of:
- the application
- the plans
- and other documents submitted with it

at *Messrs Brown and Templeman, 39 High Street, Borminster Newton, Borsetshire,* during all reasonable hours until *22 October 1990.*

Anyone who wishes to make representations about this application should write to the Council at *Slagthorpe District Council Planning Department, Town Hall, Slagthorpe, Borsetshire* by *22 October 1990.*

Signed: ~~Mary Peggoty~~

* ~~On behalf of:~~

Date: *1 October 1990*

* Delete where inappropriate

Submitting your application

Once you have completed all the necessary forms and certificates, and produced the plans for the development, you are ready to submit your application. But first you should make copies of all the documents: the number of copies will be specified in the local planning authority's guidance notes, and is likely to be four. Add one copy for your own records.

The following should be included with your application:

- the main application form (including supplementary parts where necessary)
- site plan
- drawings, plans, etc.
- the appropriate certificate of ownership (plus newspaper advertisement if necessary)
- the correct fee
- with bad neighbour developments, the appropriate certificates (plus newspaper advertisement).

A covering letter should list the enclosures.

TIP

Check carefully that you have included all the necessary documents with your application. If you leave something out, the local planning authority will have to write to you to get it. Since planning decisions are normally made monthly, your permission could be delayed for a month while the missing documents are found.

Processing the application

Your application should be acknowledged in writing within a few days, assigning it a number to be quoted in all correspondence. The acknowledgement will also tell you the date the application was received – this is the starting date for the various deadlines involved in processing your application. If there is something wrong with your application (you have sent the wrong fee, for example), you will be notified, and the receipt date will not be logged until a valid application is submitted.

Once the application is registered, you may still be asked for further information. This request may come as soon as the papers are received, or later, when officials are scrutinising them.

Consultation by the local planning authority

The first step for the local planning authority is to register the application and make a set of copies available for public consultation.

With listed buildings (see p. 93) and applications in conservation areas and other special areas (see p. 97), the local planning authority may have to publicise the application in various ways. For example, an advertisement in a local newspaper may invite the public to study the application. But even for more straightforward planning applications, the local planning authority may notify neighbours or anyone else likely to be affected. And if a development conflicts with the development plan for the area, it must be advertised in a local newspaper as a 'departure application'.

There are also a number of bodies which have to be informed of certain types of planning applications. For example, the Secretary of State has to be notified of applications within three kilometres of Windsor Castle or 800 metres of any other royal park or palace if it might affect its amenities. He also has to be told about certain 'departure applications' (see above). Water authorities have to be told about work to the bed or banks of streams (and also about a number of industrial applications which might pollute the water supplies). The Ministry of Agriculture is warned about any applications which would involve the loss of more than 20 hectares of agricultural land – and so on.

TIP

Ask how your application will be dealt with when you submit it. If it's to be dealt with by planning officers, it is likely to be regarded as an uncontentious application which can be approved provided certain conditions are met. An application which goes before the planning committee (or a sub-committee) is probably more significant or contentious, and you might need to lobby for support (or get the advice of professional planning consultants).

Where a planning committee is to take the decision, this will usually be on the basis of a report on the proposal from the chief planning officer, who will give a recommendation to accept, reject or amend it. You can normally attend such planning committee meetings, and ask to see the agenda and reports in advance under the Access to Information Act 1985. In some cases you can be denied access to papers and meetings, but you must be given a specific reason (and you could appeal on this to the Local Ombudsman – see p. 63).

If there is a third-tier local council, such as a parish council or town council (community council in Wales and Scotland), it is entitled to be informed of all planning applications in its area if it requests it.

The local planning authority decision

The responsibility for making the decision on your application rests with the local planning authority – that is, the appropriate district or occasionally the county council (although in some circumstances the application may be passed on to a higher authority – see p. 60).

Where a local council is to make the decision, authority is usually delegated to the planning committee. The planning committee will further delegate responsibility to officers (though some decisions cannot be delegated in this way). The full council normally nods through the committee's report at council meetings to approve it.

Typically, the chief planning officer will deal with just under half of all applications. The rest will be dealt with by the full planning committee or a sub-committee with full powers.

When a higher authority is involved

County councils take planning decisions on mining and waste disposal, and all planning decisions in National Parks are taken by the National Parks Authorities (see p. 98). In these cases your application will be decided on by similar procedures to those described above. The county council will also be consulted on applications which conflict 'materially' with the structure plan for the county (see p. 160) or which would hinder its implementation. And the county is also consulted on applications affecting highways.

Various government bodies must be consulted on some applications (for example, the Department of Transport where trunk roads are involved). The Secretary of State also has to be consulted about serious cases of conflict

---

TIP

If your proposal is for a major development or likely to be controversial, there are steps you can take to try to improve your chances:

- ask neighbours who support your proposal (or who are not opposed to it) to write saying so to the local planning authority – this could help balance objections from other neighbours
- seek an interview with the planning officer who covers your area before putting in your application to discuss it and find out how you can maximise your chances of success
- contact your local councillors to do the same – if the proposal seems to be a party political issue locally and your councillor's party opposes it, contact a councillor ·from another party.

---

between a planning application and the structure plan. And in very rare cases the Secretary of State can call in the application from the local planning authority so that he can decide it. Typically, this would happen with a major project of strategic importance or public concern, such as a regional shopping centre or new village.

In Scotland, regional or islands councils can also call in an application in certain circumstances.

How quickly will the decision come through?

You are supposed to get the decision on your planning application within eight weeks of the date of submission. In practice the majority of householders' applications are decided within that time-scale. Some applications take longer because they are controversial or because further information or consultation is needed – though a few take more than 13 weeks.

In some cases the delay may be to your advantage; for example, the planning officer might want to discuss some amendments with you which would allow permission to be granted. But unless the local planning authority has your agreement in writing to extend the eight-week deadline, you can appeal to the Secretary of State in the same way as if your application had been turned down (see Chapter 4 for the procedure). This isn't usually recommended, since once the case is under appeal the local planning authority can't then make a decision – and the appeal might take six months or more.

What the decision might be

If you strike lucky, the response to your application will be that full planning permission is granted without strings. You can go ahead at any time in the next five years, provided you stick to the plans you submitted. Until the work is completed, the permission can be modified or revoked by the local planning authority, although you can claim compensation if this happened (or force the local authority to buy the site). If the work is not done within five years and the permission lapses, a further application will be required to renew the planning permission.

With outline planning permission, you have up to three years to move on to the next stage of submitting a further application to get approval of the details (see p. 25).

At the other end of the spectrum is outright refusal of planning permission. More common is for permission to be granted subject to conditions about access, use, hours, materials or any of a host of relevant issues. In many cases these conditions will be acceptable (if sometimes irksome), but in others they may mean substantially altering your plans. For what to do if either of these is the outcome, see p. 63.

Reasons for planning decisions

The central principle which local planning authorities have to take into account in making their decisions is that people should be free to develop their homes and land as they wish unless there is a good reason why they shouldn't (see p. 27). This means that your application should be approved unless there is a positive reason for refusing permission.

The most important planning factor in this decision is how the application relates to the development plan. A proposal which fits in with the plan is less likely to be refused than one that doesn't – even if there are lots of objections from neighbours against it. This is why it is so important in drawing up an application to consider the plan, and tailor your proposal to fit its policies on the character of the area, the types of development it encourages and other factors, such as building materials and amenities.

But objections from people or organisations materially affected by your proposal are also important, and again this is why it is sensible to talk to neighbours first. Even if you cannot head off their objections, you may be able to show that your application does not materially affect them (for example, that it won't deprive them of an amenity).

If the decision is to turn down your application, the local planning authority must give the reasons for its decisions. You could challenge those if they were not relevant to the planning process – for example, planning permission cannot be refused because it would reduce property values in the area (or increase them).

Not happy about the result?

If you are not happy about the decision on your planning application, there is an appeals process which is explained in detail in the next chapter. But appealing is time-consuming and can be costly – and is unlikely to produce a result within much less than six months. It is always worth a second approach to the local planning authority to explore ways of getting the permission you need.

For example, relatively small changes in materials, dimensions or location may be all that is needed. Or you could propose steps to overcome objections about traffic problems or nuisance to neighbours. Can you tailor your plans to fit in better with the local plan, or to satisfy the policy objectives of the local council? A new planning application is free if submitted within 12 months.

In some cases you may feel that the problem lies in the procedure adopted by the local planning authority. For example, there was unnecessary delay in processing your application which prejudiced its success, or the local planning authority failed to do something that would have helped your application. The Local Ombudsman can investigate complaints about the way that local councils work, and perhaps recommend some restitution (or at least advise on how such maladministration could be avoided in the future).

Note that the Local Ombudsman can't examine the merits of your planning application. If you feel that the local planning authority has made the wrong decision for planning reasons, you should appeal against it to the Secretary of State

63

(see next chapter). The Local Ombudsman won't investigate a complaint if you are appealing against the decision or if you might reasonably be expected to appeal. And you must normally take the complaint to the Ombudsman (or raise it with a councillor) as quickly as possible and certainly within a year of learning about the decision.

Before making a complaint to the Local Ombudsman, you must first give the local planning authority the chance to deal with it. Contact the planning department to take it up, or write to the chief executive of the council. If you are not satisfied with the response, ask a councillor to take up your complaint (it doesn't have to be a councillor for your ward, but it must be an elected member of the body which is the planning authority for this decision). Only if you are still dissatisfied with the response can you approach the Local Ombudsman (or ask the councillor to refer your case for you).

There's a useful guide on making a complaint to the Local Ombudsman, together with a form for making the complaint, available from the Local Ombudsman's offices (addresses on p. 196).

4

APPEALING AGAINST A PLANNING DECISION

If the local planning authority refuses you the planning permission you need, or grants it with unacceptable conditions, you can appeal against the decision. You can also appeal if the local planning authority takes too long to make a decision (though this is not always advisable – see p. 61). And if you get an enforcement notice instructing you to undo some work you have done, you can appeal against that (details in Chapter 8).

The appeal procedure need not be unduly arduous or legalistic, and you can present your own case without professional help (though this may be desirable in some cases). If you have valid reasons to back your case, an appeal is well worth considering.

More information

The Department of the Environment and the Welsh Office have produced a useful guide on appealing in England and Wales: *Planning Appeals – A Guide*. This is available from the following (see p. 195 for addresses):

- *England:* the Planning Inspectorate of the Department of the Environment and Transport
- *Wales:* the Welsh Office Planning Division.

The equivalent body in Scotland is the Scottish Development Department.

The appeals process

The appeals process allows a review of the planning merits of a local planning authority decision. In theory, the appeal is to the Secretary of State: in England, the Secretary of State for the Environment; in Wales, the Secretary of State for Wales; in Scotland, the Secretary of State for Scotland. In practice, the appeal is usually handled by Civil Servants; the Secretary of State gets involved only in highly controversial cases (no more than one in thirty appeals).

Deadlines for appealing

Appeals against the decisions of a local planning authority must be made within six months of the date on the notice setting out the decision. With an appeal against delays in making a decision, it must be made within six months of the date that the decision should have been made.

Late appeals can be accepted when there is good cause for the delay. In practice, it is very rare for a late appeal to be accepted – because there are few justifications for waiting longer than six months.

Who carries out the appeal

Most appeals will be settled by an independent inspector under the direction of the Planning Inspectorate in England, the Planning Division of the Welsh Office in Wales. In Scotland appeals are settled by Reporters working for the Development Department of the Scottish Office.

There are around 200 full-time inspectors, who cover the whole range of planning appeals, including public inquiries. There is a similar number of part-time inspectors, who are normally used for written appeals only. Based throughout the country, inspectors have a variety of professional backgrounds and qualifications. Some are town planners, some are architects, and so on. They are trained to examine the evidence and make decisions in the light of planning law and precedents.

The inspectors' work is organised by the Planning Inspectorate in Bristol (by their equivalents for Wales and Scotland). You deal with the Planning Inspectorate rather than the individual inspector in making your appeal. Your appeal form must be sent to the Inspectorate, which will assemble the papers, arrange the site visit, ask you for more information the inspector requires, and so on. When the decision on the appeal is made, the letter notifying you will come from the Planning Inspectorate.

Even when an appeal is to be settled by the Secretary of State, an inspector is appointed to report on the case first. The inspector's report is passed to the regional office of the Department of the Environment for further consideration (or to the Welsh and Scottish Offices in those countries).

The appeal procedure

You can choose between two procedures for the appeal: a written appeal or a public inquiry.

A **written appeal** is made on the basis of written evidence from you, the local planning authority and any other interested party. The inspector will inspect the site, and you can be there at the time, but you cannot discuss the case with the inspector then or at any other time. A written appeal is usually settled within six months or so and no costs can be awarded against either side. This is the method chosen for four out of five appeals.

A **public inquiry** allows oral evidence to be heard and witnesses questioned – both you and the local planning authority can participate. This gives you a greater opportunity to put your case and challenge the local planning authority – useful if you want to question its case. But it can take rather longer than a written appeal – eight or nine months, say. If you lose, you may in some circumstances have to pay some or all of the other side's costs.

With appeals which the Secretary of State is to decide, he

may decide that an inquiry has to be held. In some cases you may be offered a hearing at which the main issues can be discussed on the basis of written submissions. This is more informal than a full local inquiry, and costs cannot be awarded against you.

TIP

For relatively simple appeals on the merits of a planning application, go for a written appeal – it is generally cheaper and quicker. A public inquiry is worth considering only if the evidence is complicated, you disagree with the local planning authority on some matter of fact or the case is so important to you that cost doesn't matter.

Who takes part

Two sets of people are always involved in the appeal (in addition to the inspector): you, the appellant; and the local planning authority you are appealing against. But other people or organisations may also be invited to submit evidence to the inspector where they have some sort of interest in the decision; these are known as 'interested persons'.

One group of interested persons that you have to notify of the appeal are any owners or agricultural tenants of the land involved. You had to tell them about your original application for planning permission (see p. 50); now you will have to warn them of your appeal using standard notices which come with the appeal forms. These 'Section 27 parties' (named after the relevant section of the Town and Country Planning Act 1971) are entitled to make written representations and to speak at any inquiry.

The local planning authority will also notify people and organisations who submitted views on your planning application when it was first considered. This could include the bodies which have to be notified about certain types of planning applications (see p. 58) or bodies which the local planning authority chose to notify (such as a local conservation group or, in rural areas, the parish council). It could also include neighbours notified about the planning application in the first place. The views they submitted will be forwarded to the inspector and they will be allowed to inspect your appeal and the local planning authority's reply. If they want to add to their original submission or take up points arising from the appeal, they can do so within 21 days.

With a public inquiry, you will have to put up a notice on the site. The local planning authority may also put up notices (for example, on lamp-posts), advertise the inquiry in local newspapers and notify people or organisations with an interest. These interested parties can also make submissions to the inquiry.

Should you appeal?

Although the appeals process should not daunt you, your chance of success is not high: about one in three appeals succeeds. On the other hand, if you genuinely feel that your application has been turned down on inappropriate criteria, or that the local planning authority has not recognised its planning merits, you should appeal.

The local planning authority will give reasons for its decision on your planning application when sending you notification of it. This must be your starting point in deciding whether an appeal is worthwhile. The appeal will succeed if you successfully challenge the local planning authority's reasons – for example, by showing that your development is acceptable for the site (or existing house if it is an alteration), that it accords with the development plan and that it does not conflict with national planning policy (for example, on transport or the Green Belt). If you are appealing against conditions imposed on you, you must try to show that they are unreasonable.

Factors which might help you in an appeal include:

- being able to disprove facts the local planning authority has quoted as important in making its decision

69

- finding very similar developments which have been permitted nearby (but remember that two cases are rarely completely identical)
- recent appeal decisions on similar developments which would have allowed you to go ahead (planning professionals have access to these)
- showing that the reasons for refusing planning permission clearly conflict with the development plans for the area
- evidence that planning officers' recommendations were overturned by councillors for reasons unconnected with planning
- producing expert witnesses whose views on matters of opinion or aesthetics back your application rather than the local planning authority's decision.

TIP

As an alternative to appealing, consider whether you could amend your application to get planning permission. It will involve less hassle, and the local planners may be quite happy to help you make the necessary changes to get it accepted.

Appealing against conditions

If you are appealing against conditions imposed on your planning application, you have a tricky choice to make. There are two options:

- you appeal against the local planning authority's decision – the inspector looks at the whole application and, while he could remove the conditions, he could also add to them, toughen them up or even refuse permission completely
- you go ahead with the development and put in a fresh application for planning permission to vary or remove the conditions. If this is unsuccessful, you appeal. The inspector then can't stop the development or add new conditions, only agree or disagree with your request to remove some or all of the conditions.

The first option is probably quicker, but could be a disaster if the inspector turns out to be harder than your local planning authority. Luckily, where the inspector is going to toughen up the permission, you will be given the option of withdrawing your appeal – and you could then go for the second option. But by this stage the whole process will have taken longer than if you had gone for the second option at the start.

In most cases there will be no danger of the inspector cracking down on your application – but if you think there is, get professional advice.

Help with your appeal

You don't need professional representation to handle an appeal, even if there is to be a local inquiry. You can represent yourself (as with the old rating appeals) and you may need no help to deal with relatively straightforward cases.

But with complicated cases, or if you prefer not to deal with such matters yourself, you can appoint someone else to act for you. It doesn't have to be an expert. You could ask a friend with a bent for administrative matters. But most people seeking help will want to use a professional with expertise in the planning system. And some sort of professional help is almost essential for an inquiry, which follows legalistic procedures on evidence, cross-examination, and so on.

Major developers employ architects and advisers skilled in planning matters to handle their applications and appeals. If you're using an architect, he or she should be able to advise

---

TIP

Don't appeal until you have discussed the matter with someone skilled in planning matters, even if it is just an hour with a consultant planner. An objective view could save you time and effort – and perhaps even money, as costs can be awarded against you after an inquiry.

---

you, or at least point you towards someone who can. Otherwise, you could approach a consultant chartered town planner for advice. Payment is likely to be based on the time you take up, so ask for an estimate in advance.

If this is beyond your means, there are various planning advice services up and down the country which can assist – see p. 198 for some addresses. Your local Citizens Advice Bureau may also be able to advise. Voluntary bodies will certainly give advice, but do not expect them to back you beyond that except in cases of great injustice or public interest. Note that Legal Aid is not generally available for planning cases.

TIP

Even if you decide that you have a case, look at the alternatives to appealing. You may be able to adjust your application to make it acceptable, or negotiate with the local planning authority on conditions. An appeal always means a delay of up to six months or more, so try to avoid it at all costs.

Submitting your appeal

The first step in making an appeal is to fill in the appeal forms (get them from the Planning Inspectorate, or the equivalent in Wales and Scotland – see p. 195 for addresses). Three copies must be completed (together with three sets of any enclosures): one to send off to the administrative centre, one to the local planning authority and one for your own records.

As with the original planning application, the forms ask you for details of the development, your name and address and the name and address of an agent if you are using one. You are asked which type of appeal you want: written appeal or public inquiry (see p. 67). And you must give details of the grounds for your appeal.

The reasons for appealing

The most important section of the main form deals with your grounds of appeal, where you explain why you disagree with the local planning authority. You could do this on one or more grounds:

- by challenging the facts as set out in the decision. If a photograph or diagram would help, include them
- by disputing the reasons given by the local planning authority – they must be precise, specific and relevant; if they are not, say so
- by citing details of similar developments which were allowed (give addresses)
- by offering special circumstances: if you are disabled, say, and the development relates to your particular needs.

Planning permission should not be refused merely because the development is not in line with the plans for the area. There is a further criterion, that the proposal would cause 'demonstrable harm to interests of acknowledged importance' (Department of Environment Circular 14/85). Interests of importance would include conservation, countryside protection, residential amenities and recreational facilities. When appealing, you can try to show that the interests are not of acknowledged importance or that there is no harm to the interests cited; or you might agree that there will be some harm but seek to show that the good that would follow from your proposals would outweigh any harm – the need for a doctor's surgery on an isolated estate, for example.

Make sure that you state your case fully and clearly. If there isn't enough space to set out your case clearly, continue on further sheets of paper and attach them to the forms. But don't go over the top on length – the inspector will not give way just because of the length of your statement.

Notifying owners and tenants

As with the original application for planning permission, you have to notify anyone who owns the site (including the freeholder if you are a leaseholder – see p. 52). Agricultural tenants must also be notified. In most cases you will be the sole owner(s) and you sign Certificate A, which is part of the main appeal form, to say that this is so.

But where there are other owners or agricultural tenants, you must send them standard notices warning them of your appeal. The notes which come with the appeal forms tell you what to do – follow them to the letter so that your appeal isn't held up. When you have sent out the necessary notices, you then sign the appropriate 'Section 27 Certificate' (B, C or D) and send it off with the appeal forms.

Other enclosures

In addition to the appeals form and Section 27 Certificate, you must include the following where relevant:

- a copy of your application for planning permission, together with a copy of the original Section 27 Certificate you sent off with the application
- copies of any plans, diagrams, drawings and other papers sent in with the original application
- copies of relevant correspondence (including letters to the local planning authority after you sent in your application)
- a copy of the notice you got from the local planning authority setting out its decision
- a map showing the site in relation to a local landmark that will help the inspector find it (a copy of a street map or Ordnance Survey 1:10,000 map with the map number marked on it)
- with 'bad neighbour' developments (see p. 54), copies of notices and the Section 26 Certificate you had to submit at the time of your original application
- with appeals on details of developments or approval of

conditions, a copy of the original application for planning permission, the permission as granted and the plan that was approved.

There are also two acknowledgement cards to fill in. One is returned to you when the appeal is received, giving your appeal reference number and the date the appeal is lodged; the other is sent to the local planning authority. The reference number must be quoted when writing in about your appeal or enquiring on progress by telephone.

You must send a copy of the appeal form and Section 27 Certificate to the local planning authority. You don't need to send copies of anything you have already sent to them, such as plans and diagrams. But if you are submitting anything with the appeal that the local planning authority hasn't already got a copy of, then you must send a copy too.

TIP

Give each enclosure a number or letter, and write it prominently on the top of the first sheet. Then compile a list of the enclosures, with a key to the reference number or letter. This makes it easier to refer to the various documents and to make sure that you have assembled everything you need.

The next steps

Once your appeal has been lodged, the planning authority will acknowledge receipt of it by returning to you the card you submitted with your appeal. You will then be sent a letter telling you the Case Officer who will handle the administrative side of the appeal. The Case Officer is your point of contact: you can write to him or her for information (to the room number given in the letter) or telephone him or her (again, the number is in the letter). Always quote your appeal reference number.

The exact procedure next depends on whether you have chosen a written appeal or a public inquiry – the details are below. But whichever it is, there will be some sort of exchange of documents: the local planning authority will have your appeal form with your reasons for appealing; you will be sent the authority's reply to comment on.

If, on seeing the local planning authority's reply, you decide that it is not worth going ahead, you should withdraw your appeal as quickly as possible (with an inquiry, you might incur costs if you do not withdraw in time). You may alternatively realise that changing your application marginally would lead to quick acceptance – again, withdraw your appeal quickly. To withdraw an appeal, simply ring the Case Officer and tell him or her. Confirm the withdrawal in writing, giving your appeal reference number, and copy the letter to the local planning authority.

A written appeal

Written appeals are carried out following rules in The Town and Country Planning (Appeals) (Written Representations Procedure) Regulations 1987 (SI 1987 no 701). There is a timetable for the procedure, for which the clock starts on the day the appeal is received at the Planning Inspectorate in Bristol (or the Welsh Office in Cardiff for Wales, the Scottish Development Department in Edinburgh for Scotland). This is the 'start date'.

As soon as the local planning authority receives your appeal form, it notifies interested people and organisations who need to be informed (see p. 68). The authority has five days from the start date in which to do this, and the interested parties have 28 days to submit any comments (which will be copied to both you and the local planning authority).

Exchange of papers

Your appeal form includes your reasons for appeal, and these will be your main statement of case. Within two weeks of the start date, the local planning authority has to send in to the Inspectorate the following papers, which form the basis of its case (these will be copied to you):

- a questionnaire on the planning application
- copies of correspondence with organisations or people who were consulted about the application
- any report the planning officer made to the planning committee
- relevant committee minutes
- extracts from plans or policy documents used to make the decision.

The local planning authority can also submit a statement setting out its case; this must be done within four weeks of the start date. If the authority does not intend to submit a statement, it should say so when returning the first batch of papers.

You then have 17 days from the date on the questionnaire to read the papers and comment on them. If the local planning authority puts in a statement, you have 17 days from the date of the statement. Don't comment for the sake of it: if you do decide to submit a further statement, you must send a copy to the local planning authority.

Somewhere between five and eight weeks after your appeal has been lodged, all the papers should be in – from you, the local planning authority and any interested parties. The Case Officer sends the papers to the inspector, who will study them and arrange to make a visit to the site.

The site visit

The inspector visits the site to assess what your planning application would mean for the surroundings. The inspector cannot discuss the merits of the appeal while on the visit, or even listen to you expounding your case. The only conversation the inspector will engage in is on the facts of the application – for example, the features of the site, the exact position of work, or whatever.

In view of this, the inspector would normally carry out the site visit alone, unless either of the following is the case:

- you ask to be there
- you need to be there to arrange access to the site.

If you or an agent are to be there, the local planning authority will be asked to send a representative too. And anyone else who asks will be told the date and time so that they can be present. None of these parties can discuss the case with the inspector on the visit – you are all bound to silence on the merits of the appeal. Arranging dates for you to be present can sometimes delay the appeal, but if there is a feature of the site to which you wish to draw attention, being present may be essential.

The site visit is the last stage of the procedure before the inspector makes his or her decision. For how that is announced – and what you can do about it – see p. 83.

Late submissions

If something comes to light after the exchanges of documents, you may still be able to submit a further statement. The Planning Inspectorate has discretion to accept late representations, but if it agrees to this the appeal will be delayed, as copies must be sent to the local planning authority for comment.

Try to avoid late submissions by including everything in the main exchange of papers. But if powerful new facts or arguments do turn up, a late submission should be made.

Public inquiry

Public inquiries are governed by rules set out in The Town and Country Planning Appeals (Determination by Inspectors) (Inquiries Procedure) Rules 1988 (SI 1988 no 945). If the Secretary of State is going to make the decision, then the rules are as set out in The Town and Country Planning (Inquiries Procedure) Rules 1988 (SI 1988 no 944).

The clock for the inquiry timetable starts from the 'relevant date'. This is the date on which the Planning Inspectorate sends you a letter saying that there will be an inquiry (a copy of this goes to the local planning authority). The inquiry will normally be held within 20 weeks of the relevant date (22 weeks if the Secretary of State is making the decision). You and the local planning authority will be consulted on the date, but each of you can refuse only one date (for example, if you're on holiday). You are entitled to 28 days' written notice of the date; in some circumstances you may be offered a date earlier than 28 days, which you can refuse if it is not convenient.

Note that the Inspectorate may suggest an informal hearing rather than a full public inquiry. This can speed things up and may be less costly for you – see p. 82.

Before the inquiry

To speed up the inquiry, written evidence and submissions are exchanged in advance. Your grounds for appeal are already set out in the appeal form. The local planning authority must send you a statement of its case, together with any documents or plans, within six weeks of the relevant date. These will also be available for the public to inspect.

You are then required to produce your own statement of case no later than nine weeks from the relevant date. You send this to the Planning Inspectorate, the local planning authority and any other parties to whom you have been told to send it (for example, interested amenity groups or neighbours who have objected).

If any statements are to be read at the inquiry, or people called to read statements, the statements must be exchanged before the inquiry. Again, copies must be sent to the Planning Inspectorate and the local planning authority not later than three weeks before the inquiry is due to start (or three weeks before the evidence will be given if that is later).

In some cases it will emerge that a government department or local authority has expressed a view on your application – opposing it or recommending tough conditions. You can ask the Planning Inspectorate to arrange for a representative of that body to attend the inquiry so that you can question him or her. The same applies where the Ministry of Agriculture, Fisheries and Food has commented on an application for the development of agricultural land, or the Health and Safety Inspectors have commented on a proposal that involves storing dangerous materials. Your request must be in writing at least two weeks before the start of the inquiry.

Finally, you will be sent a notice to display at the site advertising the inquiry. If you are unable to do this (because you don't own the land, say), the local planning authority will put the notice up prominently nearby. The local planning authority will be asked to publicise the inquiry in other ways, by telling local newspapers, for example, and notifying anyone who may be affected by your plans.

Pre-inquiry meeting

With complicated cases the inspector may call a pre-inquiry meeting. This enables the parties to introduce themselves, the procedure and running order to be agreed and any requests for further information to be made.

The inquiry

The inspector presides over the inquiry, and he or she should follow the procedures set out in the Inquiries Procedure Rules (if you want to study these, you can get them from HMSO – see p. 196). He or she begins by stating the purpose of the inquiry; each side then gives their names and lists the witnesses they intend to call. The inspector asks if there are other interested parties who would like to say something. The rest of the inquiry then goes as follows unless the inspector decides otherwise:

1. You (or your representative) are asked to present your case. You should summarise the history of the application, the salient points you wish to make and the arguments in favour of upholding your appeal. You can call witnesses if you wish (the inspector can in exceptional circumstances ask them to give evidence on oath). Both you and the witnesses can be questioned by the local planning authority and by the inspector, or by any other owners of the site. After this, you have an opportunity to ask your witnesses further questions.

2. The local planning authority then presents its case. Often this is done by a solicitor who works for the council. You can question the local planning authority and its witnesses (as can any other owners of the site). The local planning authority's witnesses will usually include planning officers or – where a committee overturned officers' recommendations – councillors on the planning committee. They may also call representatives of government departments or other public bodies.

3. Next come other interested parties (often called third parties) who may speak but not call witnesses. If there are other owners of the site, they come first. Then neighbours, local amenity groups, and so on (they can be represented by a solicitor or other professional). The inspector may be prepared to read out written submissions at this stage. If you have asked for a representative of a public body to be present because it has expressed a view on your application, he or she can be questioned now. The inspector can allow these people to question you or you to question them – if you want to challenge what they say, be sure to ask for permission to do so.

4. Finally, you can make a closing statement, summarising your case and dealing with points which have arisen during the inquiry. You must not introduce new material at this stage – merely draw together the threads of what has gone before.

The inspector then closes the inquiry. If new evidence emerges later, you can submit it (with copies to the local planning authority). But as this will involve more toing and froing, and even the reopening of the inquiry, it is not recommended other than in exceptional circumstances.

Site visit

The inspector will normally visit the site before the inquiry to familiarise himself with it. You or the local planning authority can ask the inspector to make a formal visit to the site during the inquiry or after it. As with written appeals, you can be present, as can the local planning authority, but the inspector will not listen to arguments about the merits of the appeal during the visit (see p. 77).

A hearing

In some cases where you have requested an inquiry, it may be obvious that a full public inquiry would be a waste of time and effort. For example, there may be no witnesses to call and no major controversy involved in the application. The Planning Inspectorate can offer you a less formal hearing instead of an inquiry, which could speed things up (as well as saving on costs).

At a hearing the inspector leads a discussion of the main issues, inviting each side to make their points (normally without legal representation). Different rules apply from those involved in an inquiry – they are set out in the Code of Practice for Hearings you will be sent when a hearing is arranged. Both sides set out their cases in writing and exchange them at least three weeks before the hearing. There are no witnesses and you will always get the chance of having the last word.

The decision about accepting the offer of a hearing is yours: apart from perhaps speeding things up, it could save you money (especially if costs are awarded against you after an inquiry – see below). Indeed, you can propose that your appeal be conducted at a hearing rather than at an inquiry, though only the Inspectorate can give the go-ahead.

The decision

In most cases the inspector makes the decision, which is passed to you in a letter around four weeks after the inquiry or the site visit. This sets out the proposal, the planning issues and the decision on the appeal. The inspector will set out the main arguments for and against your application and explain the reasons for his or her decision. A copy will be sent to the local planning authority and anyone else who has asked for one.

The inspector has a number of options:

- to completely reject your appeal
- to completely accept your appeal, so that you have the planning permission you applied for
- to accept your appeal in part – that is, give you planning permission subject to conditions.

Advance notice

With an inquiry or hearing, the inspector may offer to let you know the decision on your appeal in advance. Both you and the local planning authority have to give your permission, since, once you have agreed, no further submissions can be made.

An Advance Notice of Decision (AND) usually comes out within a day or two of the end of the inquiry or hearing, letting you know the decision. The formal decision letter follows as normal with the detail about the decision.

Where the Secretary of State decides

In the three per cent of cases that the Secretary of State decides, the inspector does not make the final decision. Instead, he or she submits a report to the Secretary of State, including details of the site gathered on the site visit. The inspector normally offers conclusions on the issues raised by the appeal and recommends allowing the appeal or dismissing it.

The Secretary of State can look at new evidence, take expert opinion or consider evidence not raised at the inquiry. He may also disagree with the inspector on the facts of the case. If the Secretary of State proposes to reject the inspector's recommendation on these grounds, he must tell you, the local planning authority and any other owners of the site. You then have 21 days in which to make written representations or ask for the inquiry to be reopened.

Once the Secretary of State has made a decision, it will be notified to you, the local planning authority and any other owners of the site. The inspector's report will usually be included – if it isn't, you can ask for a copy. Anyone else who has asked to be told of the decision will also be sent it.

Costs

Both sides meet their own costs with a written appeal or a hearing. This is also the norm with a public inquiry, but in some circumstances one side can be made to pay some or all of the other side's costs.

Costs are only awarded where the inspector (or the Secretary of State) is convinced that the one side has behaved unreasonably, forcing the other side to incur the costs: for example, if you produced evidence at the inquiry that hadn't been aired before (which forced an adjournment and further delay) or insisted on appealing in a hopeless case. Equally, you could ask for costs if the local planning authority has behaved unreasonably and put you to expense – for example, if it could not justify the decision you are appealing against.

Costs are awarded only if you or the other side asks for them at the inquiry (you can claim later only if there is a good reason for the delay). You will not normally get all your costs – only the extra incurred because of the other side's unreasonable behaviour.

For more about costs in England and Wales, see *Awards of Costs Following Planning Appeals – a Guide for Appellants*, available from the Planning Inspectorate and the Welsh Office.

Further appeal

The decision of the Secretary of State (or his inspector) is final, and there is no further appeal on planning grounds. But there are various ways to challenge the decision if you think that the appeals procedure was not followed or that you have been denied natural justice.

The High Court

You can challenge an appeal decision on a point of law in the High Court (the Court of Session in Scotland). You will have to show that the inspector or the Secretary of State exceeded his or her powers in some way, or that the way the procedure was handled denied you a fair hearing. The challenge must be entered within six weeks of the date of issue of the decision letter. If the challenge is successful, the High Court will force the case to be reconsidered (it cannot overturn the decision).

A High Court challenge is expensive, though you may be eligible for Legal Aid (ask your local Citizens Advice Bureau). Legal advice is essential.

The Ombudsman

The Parliamentary Commissioner for Administration – the Ombudsman – can investigate unfair treatment by national government departments such as the Planning Inspectorate and the Department of the Environment. He has no power to overturn the decision, or to comment on the merits of the appeal – even where he finds that there was a factual mistake. But if he judges that there has been a case of serious maladministration, the department involved will be under pressure to make some restitution. This may be no more than an apology, but in some well-publicised cases there has been payment of compensation. At the very least, administration is improved to avoid recurrences in the future – so you could help future appellants.

To get the Parliamentary Ombudsman to take up your case, you must persuade an MP to refer it to him, normally within a year of discovering the maladministration. Approach your own MP first with details; if your own MP will not take it on, any MP can do it. A leaflet called *Can the Parliamentary Ombudsman help you?* is available from the Ombudsman's office (address on p. 196).

The Council on Tribunals

This council is an independent government-funded body which considers, to ensure fair play, how all sorts of official tribunals and inquiries organise themselves. If you have a complaint about the way your appeal was handled, the council may take up the matter if it thinks that the matter reveals a flaw in the appeals process that needs to be rectified. This won't alter the decision, and the council does not consider the planning merits of your case. Addresses on p. 196.

=== 5 ===

LIVING IN A SPECIAL BUILDING OR AREA

The rules outlined in Chapters 1 and 2 about when to apply for planning permission may not apply to houses which are 'listed' as being of special architectural or historic interest. And there are areas of both town and countryside which have special planning rules in order to conserve their character, natural or man-made.

There are useful circulars from the three Secretaries of State on listed buildings and conservation areas (all available from HMSO Books – see p. 196).

Listed buildings

Britain's architectural heritage is given some protection by the system of listing buildings 'of special architectural or historic interest'. Most listed buildings are houses – including farms and castles – and their outbuildings (stables, barns, summerhouses, lodges, and so on). But any structure can be covered, and factories, warehouses, shops and offices have all been listed. So too have milestones, war memorials, bridges, walls, lych-gates and even a stone track in Whitby. And over a thousand of the old red telephone boxes, designed by Sir Gilbert Scott, are on the list.

Once a building has been listed, it is against the law to demolish it or to alter it without getting listed building consent. This doesn't replace the normal planning regulations: you may need planning permission as well. In general it is harder to get the go-ahead to develop a listed building, and many of the operations which do not require planning permission (including internal alterations and decorating the outside) may require listed building consent.

A further advantage of listing is that local planning authorities must take extra care when considering planning applications that affect the *setting* of a listed building. This might cover buildings and land some way from the listed building if they contribute to its character and charm.

Who lists buildings?

The responsibility for listing buildings rests with the Secretary of State. In most cases a building becomes listed because the local planning authority has asked the Secretary of State to list it. But the Secretary of State can list buildings on his own initiative, and often does so as a result of lobbying by individuals or special interest groups.

Local planning authorities can also use the listing process to stop the demolition or alteration of a building. If they have asked the Secretary of State to list a building, they can issue a Building Preservation Order to protect it from demolition or alteration while the request is considered. The Building Preservation Order remains in force for a maximum of six months, or until the Secretary of State issues his decision if that is sooner. While the order is in force, the building is treated as if it were listed, requiring listed building consent where necessary (see p. 90).

Which buildings are listed?

The basic criterion for listing is that the building should be 'of special architectural or historic interest'. This doesn't mean that the building has to be beautiful – well-known eyesores have been listed because they are typical of an architectural period or illustrate the work of a certain architect. And listing can cover a group of buildings, so that a house of no special interest might be listed because to demolish it would spoil the group effect.

A building can also be listed because of features fixed to it or within its curtilage. So a house with an unappealing exterior could be listed because it has Roman remains incorporated into its footings or a medieval frieze on an inside wall or wood panelling of particular merit. Such features must be fixed to the building in such a way as to be part of it.

Well over half a million buildings are now listed, including all buildings built before 1700. Most buildings put up between 1700 and 1840 are listed, as are any of definite quality from 1840 to 1914. Some more recent buildings have also been listed, including good examples of inter-war building such as the Egyptian-style Hoover factory in Perivale and BBC Broadcasting House. And a few post-war buildings have now been added to the list, including the 1950s Trades Union Congress headquarters in London's Bloomsbury, the Royal Festival Hall and the former *Financial Times* building, Bracken House.

Listed buildings are classified in one of three grades:

- Grade I – for buildings of 'exceptional interest' (only about one per cent of the total fall into this grade)
- Grade II* – for some 20,000 buildings of 'particular importance and perhaps containing outstanding features'
- Grade II – for buildings of 'special interest which warrant every effort being made to preserve them'.

In Scotland there are three grades (A, B and C) but with rather different definitions.

How to find out if your home is listed

You should find out that your home is listed when you buy it, from the searches you or your solicitor carry out as part of conveyancing (if the previous owner does not tell you). The local planning authority will have recorded the listing on its records for the building, as will the Land Registry for registered property. If you are buying a listed house, it is more important than normal to check that any alterations have had the necessary permission, since even quite small changes may have to be undone if listed building consent is not given.

If your house is about to be listed, the first you may hear is when the local planning authority notifies you of the *fait accompli*. You won't necessarily be told first – the Secretary of State doesn't have to give you advance notice – and you cannot appeal against the decision. The only way to challenge listing is by appealing against refusal of listed building consent (see p.94).

Owners of listed buildings have to keep them in reasonable repair (in addition to meeting the special planning regulations). The local planning authority can force the owner to look after it, or even compulsorily purchase it. Grants may be available for certain repairs, especially with Grade I buildings: ask the local planning authority or amenity and conservation groups. VAT is not payable on alterations to listed buildings which have been given listed building consent.

Getting protection from listing

If you want to develop a building and are worried that it may be listed in the future, you can ask the Secretary of State for an undertaking not to list it in the near future (this does not apply in Scotland). This provision is necessary because it could effectively wreck a development if the building is listed after work has started (and cost you a lot of money).

Anyone who has applied for or been granted planning permission for development which involves the alteration or demolition of a building can apply for a certificate of immunity from listing for that building. The Secretary of State doesn't have to issue one – indeed, applying for a certificate may lead to the building being listed. But once a certificate has been issued, it guarantees that the building will not be listed during the following five years, nor will a Building Preservation Order be issued on it.

When to apply for listed building consent

You must apply to the local planning authority for listed building consent if you want to carry out any of the following:

- demolition of any part of a listed building
- extensions to a listed building, whatever their size
- alterations to a listed building which would affect its character as a building of special architectural or historic interest (including attaching a satellite dish)
- to demolish or alter any object or structure attached to the listed building or within its curtilage
- put advertising on the outside or inside of a listed building.

These go much further than the definition of development for which planning permission is needed. For example, you don't need planning permission for internal works in a house which is not listed. But it will often be the case that internal alterations would affect the special architectural or historic interest of a listed house.

Painting the outside of most houses is permitted development for which permission is not normally needed (see p. 20). With a listed building, painting the outside – or even just the woodwork – could completely alter its appearance and thus require listed building consent.

The special planning rules for listed buildings apply to all buildings within their curtilage erected before 1948. This includes structures in the garden or courtyard (stables, sheds, barns, walls and gates) and even other buildings in the same group (see p. 88).

If in doubt about whether you need to apply for listed building consent, the general rule is to apply. You can't get a ruling that a particular alteration doesn't need listed building consent, as you can with planning permission (see p. 26). And just asking the advice of your local planning authority isn't enough: the advice of a planning officer is not binding on the authority. Only by applying for formal listed building consent can you get a decision which cannot be overturned later.

Note that there are exemptions to the listed buildings rules for Crown properties and the Church of England. So listed churches, for example, can be altered as long as they are still places of worship.

91

Planning permission for listed buildings

Applying for listed building consent doesn't cover you for planning permission. If you need planning permission for whatever it is you want to do, then you must apply for that separately at the same time.

And some types of development which are permitted development for ordinary houses aren't allowed without planning permission for listed buildings:

- erecting or altering fences, walls or gates – whatever their height
- putting up an outbuilding of more than 10 cubic metres in volume.

Applying for listed building consent

Your local planning authority will have special forms for applying for listed building consent, which you must complete and sign. Most local planning authorities have a specialist conservation officer who will give you advice and suggest steps that might help you do what you want to achieve. There is no fee to pay when applying for listed building consent.

Send with the application form:

- a plan of the site edged in red, as with applications for planning permission (and using a similar scale map – see p. 48)
- plans and drawings of alterations or the extension with enough detail to give a clear picture of what you propose to do
- as an optional extra, photographs of relevant parts of the house, such as the side where an extension is to be built or the parts to be altered.

As with applications for planning permission, you have to tell any owners about your application (an owner is anyone with a freehold interest or a leasehold interest with more than seven years left to run of the lease). The same applies if you share ownership of the building – the other owners must be informed. If you cannot notify an owner (for example, because you don't know the address), you have to take out an advertisement in a local newspaper informing the owner of your application. The application form must be accompanied by a certificate saying that you have taken the appropriate steps to inform the owner (with a copy of the newspaper advertisement if that was the method used). The precise wording of the notice, advertisement and certificates is set out in the planning legislation, and further details should come with the application forms for listed building consent.

How your application is processed

The local planning authority will normally acknowledge receipt of your application for listed building consent, register it and make it available for public inspection. The only exception would be where the local planning authority decides that listed building consent is not required: if it returns your application on these grounds, you cannot later be stopped or forced to undo the alterations.

If the local planning authority proposes to give consent to demolish a listed building, it must notify the Secretary of State, who has 28 days to decide whether or not to call in the application. This is not unusual with major work: the Secretary of State then makes the decision, with the local planning authority able to take part in the hearing. There is likely to be a public inquiry – see p. 78 for how this works.

If the application is not called in, the local planning authority can go ahead with making a decision on it. With most listed building consent applications, the local planning authority will advertise the proposals, so that members of the general public can be alerted to them. The only exceptions are alterations to the interior of a Grade II building – all others have to be advertised. The advertisement will normally be in a local newspaper, and a notice stuck up on or near the building affected for at least seven days. These will state that the plans can be inspected by the general public for up to 21 days and that representations to the authority must be made within that time.

The local planning authority also has to tell the Historic Buildings and Monuments Commission (English Heritage) about applications for all listed buildings in Greater London and Grade I and Grade II* listed buildings outside London. The Royal Fine Art Commission is often consulted. If a listed building in England is to be demolished, the Ancient Monuments Society, the Council for British Archaeology, the Georgian Group, the Victorian Society and the Society for the Protection of Ancient Buildings must also be notified.

The local planning authority is supposed to make its decision within eight weeks of the application being submitted; your agreement should be sought if it takes longer. If consent is given, the local planning authority can set conditions, for example on the use of particular materials or the protection of a special feature. All listed building consents are issued with the proviso that they lapse if not carried out within five years.

If the consent is to demolish a listed building, the local planning authority has to inform the Royal Commission on the Historical Monuments of England. Demolition cannot begin until the Royal Commission has had a month to record the building, by photographing it, for instance, or indicated that it does not wish to do so.

There are some differences in the procedures for Wales and Scotland – ask the local planning authority for advice.

Appeals

If your application is turned down, or granted with unacceptable conditions, you can appeal to the Secretary of State. You can also appeal if the local planning authority fails to give its decision within the eight-week deadline. You could appeal on the grounds that the building is not of special architectural or historic interest (as noted above, this is really the only way to appeal against listing in the first place).

The appeal hearing will be similar to those for planning applications (see Chapter 4), with both you and the local planning authority able to present your cases. You can challenge the appeal finding only in the High Court – and then only on the same grounds as for planning appeals (see p. 85).

Ancient monuments

There are 13,000 ancient monuments in Britain, ranging from the oldest structures such as Stonehenge to more modern edifices like barns, bridges and churches. The procedures for ancient monuments are set out in the Ancient Monuments and Archaeological Areas Act 1979 (available from HMSO bookshops). They are broadly similar to those for listed buildings (for example, permission is needed for demolition). But application for permission must be made to the Secretary of State direct, rather than the local planning authority.

Some listed buildings are also ancient monuments: in this case the procedure for planning is that set out in ancient monument legislation rather than for listed buildings. The same applies if the monument is in a conservation area (see below) – there is no need to get conservation area consent as well.

Living in a special area

Britain's heritage consists of much more than just individual houses and buildings. Whole villages and areas in towns and cities remain well preserved in their original form – whether it be Cotswolds villages, the Georgian crescents of Bath or the Victorian estates of big cities. The countryside itself is under pressure from the increasing desire of people to move out of urban areas and the growth in leisure time. The planning system has recognised this by providing for stricter regulation of development in special areas.

Conservation areas

Conservation areas are areas of special architectural or historic interest, the character of which it is desirable to preserve or enhance. Local planning authorities are under an obligation to assess which parts of their territory might qualify, and to designate them as conservation areas. There are well over 5000 conservation areas. For details of how they are designated, see p. 147.

If a building in a conservation area is listed, then the rules for listed buildings apply. But for houses in conservation areas which aren't listed, there are special planning regulations:

- trees cannot be felled, topped, lopped or wilfully damaged unless six weeks' notice is given to the local planning authority, which can then decide whether to issue a Tree Preservation Order to cover it (though if the tree is dead, dying or dangerous, it can be dealt with as for trees without a Preservation Order – see p. 23)
- there are stricter rules about the minor alterations or small extensions you can build without planning permission – see below
- demolition – even partial – requires special conservation area consent (see p. 97).

An 'Article 4 direction' (see p. 98) can further restrict the work that is allowed to be done to the outside of buildings it covers without planning permission. This can include re-painting in a different colour.

When planning permission isn't needed

As with houses outside conservation areas, you can go ahead with minor alterations and build small extensions without applying for planning permission – within strict limits. Blanket permission is given in advance for certain types of 'permitted development' in conservation areas under the General Development Order (see p. 31). But the limits are even stricter on what is permitted than for ordinary houses:

- extensions must not take the volume of the house more than 50 cubic metres over the original volume, or 10 per cent of the original volume if that is more, with an overall maximum increase of 115 cubic metres. These limits apply whether the house is terraced or not
- all loft or roof extensions need an application for planning permission – whatever their size or design
- you can't put on stone cladding, external panelling or tiling without applying for planning permission
- you must apply for planning permission to put up any outbuilding more than 10 cubic metres in volume
- any outbuilding over 10 cubic metres in volume counts as part of the house, regardless of its distance from the house (that is, it is included even if it is more than five metres from the house). This means that its volume must be included in calculating the volume of the house and any extensions.

An 'Article 4 direction' can withdraw some or all of these permitted developments – see p. 98.

These stricter rules on permitted development also apply to houses in National Parks, Areas of Outstanding Natural Beauty and some other beauty-spots – see p. 98.

TIP

If in doubt about whether you need planning permission in a conservation area, ask your local planning authority for guidance. If it's still not clear, get a Section 53 determination (see p. 26).

Conservation area consent

Demolition of buildings in a conservation area requires conservation area consent unless they are covered by some other protection (that is, are listed buildings or ancient monuments). This also applies to demolishing part of a building – for example, to make way for an extension.

The only exceptions are:

- buildings of a total volume of less than 115 cubic metres
- a gate, wall, fence or railing less than one metre high beside a road or path, or less than two metres high elsewhere
- buildings you are required to demolish by statutory order (for example, as part of a road-widening scheme).

Getting conservation area consent involves much the same process as getting listed building consent (see p. 92). The main differences are that the Secretary of State doesn't get involved unless you appeal (he cannot call in a case to rule on it himself); and you don't have to get the go-ahead from the Royal Commission on the Historical Monuments of England before proceeding with demolition.

Article 4 directions

The local planning authority can issue a direction which withdraws some or all of the permitted developments which are normally allowed without submitting a planning application. These are known as 'Article 4 directions' after the clause of the General Development Order which gives the power. The direction will specify which of the permitted developments are withdrawn, and the area it applies to; the approval of the Secretary of State will normally be needed. If you then wish to carry out one of the developments covered by the direction, you will have to apply for planning permission.

National Parks

There are ten National Parks in England and Wales, ranging from Dartmoor in the south and Snowdonia in Wales to the Lake District in the north. They are usually large areas of mountain and moorland designated as such to conserve and enhance their natural beauty and to promote their enjoyment by the public. Though not officially a National Park, the Norfolk and Suffolk Broads are very similar in their administration and planning system.

In recognition of the special importance of conserving National Parks, all planning decisions within them are taken in consultation with a single National Park Authority, covering the whole area. The Secretary of State appoints a third of the members of these National Park Authorities, with the rest nominated by local councils. This concentration at the level of the park as a whole, rather than at the more local district council level, enables all decisions within the park to reflect uniform standards, and prevents developers playing one district council off against another.

There is also special funding for the National Parks, in recognition of their national importance. Three-quarters of their budget comes from the Department of the Environment, and a national quango, the Countryside Commission, advises on and co-ordinates their work.

To promote the twin aims of protection and enjoyment, each authority produces a National Park Management Plan, which sets out proposals to protect the landscape and increase provision for the enjoyment of the public. Any development in a National Park will be considered very carefully, to preserve its beauty. And while minor alterations and small extensions are allowed without applying for planning permission as 'permitted development', the stricter rules set out above for houses in conservation areas also apply to National Parks.

In addition, it is more difficult to get consent for outdoor advertisements in a National Park – especially if they are illuminated.

Areas of Outstanding Natural Beauty

In addition to the National Parks, there are many Areas of Outstanding Natural Beauty (AONBS), such as the Weald of Kent and the North Yorkshire Moors. These are areas with similar landscape qualities to the National Parks, but are often smaller. The local planning authority in an AONB is encouraged to preserve and enhance the area's natural beauty, but doesn't have the power of a National Parks Authority to provide facilities for public enjoyment. The stricter rules for permitted development which apply in conservation areas (see p. 97) also apply in AONBS.

Other special areas

Other special areas include Heritage Coasts, Coastal Protection Areas and Environmentally Sensitive Areas (of farmland). In these cases the special features which have led to their designation are considered important in dealing with planning applications.

PART 2

Planning in Your Neighbourhood

=== 6 ===

YOUR RIGHTS AS A HOUSEHOLDER

The Englishman's home is his castle . . . or is it? Earlier chapters have looked at householders' rights when it comes to altering their own homes – but what sort of protection is there if a neighbour starts to behave in a way that infringes your enjoyment of your home? This chapter looks at your rights as a householder against the actions of others.

A clash of rights

As a householder, you have rights over your property. Your neighbours enjoy similar rights over theirs. The problem arises when exercising one set of rights means that someone else cannot fully exercise theirs.

To take a simple example, you may feel that you have the right to listen to music on your stereo at concert volume – indeed, that being able to do so is one of the main pleasures of home ownership. A neighbour may feel that your hobby infringes his right to peace and quiet – especially if he works shifts and has to sleep during the daytime. Good neighbours will find a way of resolving this clash of rights, in which each gives up some of their absolute entitlement: you may agree to confine your listening to certain hours or move your hi-fi into a different room; your neighbour might take some elementary sound-proofing steps (especially if there are other noise problems locally) and let you know at which times in the near future he will be sleeping.

In real life there are few absolute rights – rights that you can exercise regardless of their effects on others. One person exercising his or her rights often means curtailing the rights of another: the civilised solution is to negotiate so that everyone makes an acceptable sacrifice of some of their rights to be able to live together congenially. It will be much easier to resolve disputes if at the outset it is recognised that all parties may have to give a little. Standing firm on the pure ground of rights may triumph in the long run – but the cost in human relations could make it a pyrrhic victory.

Always remember that the law is imperfect on many such matters. You may feel that you have a 'right' to this or that – but there may be no right in a legal sense. A neighbour's dog may bring on your dust allergy, and a good neighbour would probably keep a dog away from your fence when you are in the garden. But you have no right to make the neighbour do so, and you are much more likely to persuade your neighbour to co-operate if you avoid banging on about rights.

TIP

Good relations with neighbours are rarely based on enforcement of legal rights: tact and persuasion should always be tried at great length first. Of course, many people find that there is no alternative with bad neighbours but to resort to the law – but it should be the last resort.

Neighbours' developments

Disputes often arise because people wish to do something to their property which neighbours do not like. In many cases you are powerless to do anything about such developments: unless it's listed or in a conservation area or some other special planning area, the house next door can be painted bright purple with green spots without your neighbours needing permission (see p. 20).

But if planning permission is needed (or listed building or conservation area consent), you can oppose the application.

For details of how to do this, see Chapter 7. And in other cases you may be able to prevent neighbours from making certain changes.

When you can't object

Broadly, you can't object to a neighbour doing something that doesn't need planning permission unless it infringes either your right to light or a covenant on their home – see below.

What can be done without planning permission is described in detail in Chapter 2. For most houses no planning permission is needed for the following, provided certain conditions are met:

- painting and decorating – inside or out
- internal alterations
- small porches away from the road (not in Scotland)
- garden sheds, aviaries and swimming-pools
- walls and fences up to certain heights
- loft extensions, within limits (not in Scotland)
- extensions and garages, within limits
- a satellite aerial
- using the property for business purposes which do not occupy more than one room or attract callers
- hard standing or drives (not in Scotland)
- converting flats back into a house
- demolition.

The rules are different for flats and maisonettes – see p. 31. While internal decorations and alterations may be allowed, most of the developments listed above would need planning permission.

There are also stricter rules for listed buildings and houses in conservation areas and other special planning areas (see Chapter 5). For example, work which would affect the external appearance of such houses usually requires permission – this includes painting or stone cladding. Alterations to the inside of listed buildings may need permission. And even

105

where extensions can be built without permission, the limits on size, etc. are stricter.

If a neighbour goes ahead with one of these types of permitted development, there's little you can do about it unless you can prove that planning permission was needed. For example, an extension needs planning permission if it increases the size of the property by more than a certain amount in relation to its original volume (see p. 33) – if you can show that it does, then planning permission is needed. And no part of the extension within two metres of the boundary of the plot should be higher than four metres; again, if you find it is, planning permission must be sought.

However, a neighbour who has done something that requires planning permission without consent won't necessarily have to undo it. The neighbour could apply for planning permission retrospectively, which at least gives you the opportunity to oppose it (see Chapter 7). But permission may well be granted, especially if any infringement of the size rules is insignificant. Only if permission is refused, or granted subject to conditions which require substantial rebuilding, will the neighbour have to undo some or all of the work.

Your right to light

There is no automatic right to daylight in your home, but you may have acquired a 'right to light' by virtue of the passage of time. If you have acquired such rights, you may be able to stop a neighbour building something which would deprive you of light even if planning permission has been given. Note that this isn't a planning law; it is a separate legal provision dating from before modern planning laws were passed.

The right to light applies if you can show that your house has enjoyed a certain level of light uninterrupted for at least 20 years (in Scotland, the length of time is not specified). You are then entitled to sufficient natural light to make your house comfortable to live in. It doesn't apply to your garden (though it does apply to greenhouses).

To enforce your right to light, you take whoever is infringing it to the County Court. Having proved that you have acquired such rights, you must then show that the light which remains is insufficient. It is not enough merely to show that light has been lost, or that now you don't get as much sun as you used to. You have to demonstrate that there is no longer enough light for your enjoyment of the property. And the amount that is needed depends on the use of the room: a bedroom or bathroom would need less light than a living-room, for example.

If you succeed in your case, the court can force the removal of the structure obscuring your light (or alterations to stop blocking it). Where the loss of light is not serious, the court may suggest compensation instead.

Note that even if you cannot claim a right to light, you may still be able to oppose developments which reduce your light if they require planning permission.

Covenants on development

If your area is built on land which has restrictive covenants applying to it, you may be able to use them to stop development out of character with the neighbourhood – even when planning permission has been granted.

Restrictive covenants are private restrictions in the deeds of houses or land, usually imposed by the original developer but which apply to the current owner. Each owner is required to agree to impose the same covenants on anyone they sell the house to (indeed, they can impose further covenants at the time of the sale). Covenants can restrict the number of dwellings per acre or stop the land being put to particular uses. They may ban infilling (splitting a garden to create a second plot for housing) or dividing a house into flats. They can stop you building large outhouses or garages, hanging washing outdoors, putting up TV aerials, erecting hedges or fences on open-plan estates or even repainting the outside of the house other than in certain colours. Provided you can find out about them, you may be able to enforce them and stop unsuitable development – even if planning permission has been given.

The difficulty is to find out what covenants apply. Only the owner has access to the deeds or the entries on the Land Register. But houses built at the same time on an estate by the same developer usually have the same covenants, so other owners can consult their deeds. If you think that there are covenants which can be used to stop unsuitable developments, tell the developers (usually only neighbours and other residents can enforce them). Legal advice may be sensible to see what the scope is for using the covenants to protect your area.

There are ways round covenants, including insurance for the developers. But the threat of invoking covenants may be enough to see the developers off.

Noise

Noise is not a planning issue unless someone is applying for permission for a development that would create more noise in an area. But a noisy neighbour can be as much of a blot on your landscape as an eyesore of an extension, and there are three remedies open to you:

- complain to the council
- complain direct to the Magistrates' Court (or, in Scotland, the Sheriff Court)
- take action under the civil law – that is, take your neighbour to the County Court.

Noise is rather less tangible than a building or a trade, so it is often harder to resolve noise disputes to the satisfaction of all sides. As with other disputes with neighbours, a few words and a bit of give and take may be the simplest and cheapest solution. But noise from neighbours can destroy your enjoyment of your home, and, when negotiation fails, certain remedies can be used.

Note that if the noise comes from a factory, builder's yard or other type of business, you may not be able to stop the noise. A notice or order will not be issued if a commercial or industrial concern can show that the best practicable means' to avoid making noise were used. So if the equipment is well maintained and the usual noise reduction precautions are taken, you may not be able to do much about the noise.

TIP

If you're affected by noise, keep a diary recording the nuisance – it could help speed up resolving the problem. Note down the date, time, duration, intensity, type and anything else that would help establish the nuisance. Also record the effects on you (disturbed sleep, say, or wakened children). And get statements from neighbours to back this up, plus notes from doctors, teachers, etc. saying what the effects are.

Complaining to the council

If noise becomes a nuisance, local councils have the power to serve a notice on the person making it which deals with the nuisance in one of the following ways:

- the notice forbids the person making the noise altogether
- the notice restricts the noise to certain levels
- the notice restricts the person making the noise to certain times of the day (normal working hours, for example).

The council has to satisfy itself that the noise does add up to a nuisance (which may take some time to establish). Once the notice has been served, the neighbour can be taken to court if it is not complied with. The maximum fine is £2000, plus £50 a day for each day that the noise continues.

The council department to contact is the Environmental Health Department of the district council (or, in London, the borough council). Some councils have special noise officers on call at busy times like Saturday night. But in some areas there are so many complaints that it could take a long time for yours to be dealt with.

Complaining direct to the Magistrates' Court

It's advisable to get a solicitor to represent you before making approaches to the Magistrates' or Sheriff Court. If you can persuade the magistrates that the noise is a nuisance, they will make an order, with the same consequences as a council notice. In Scotland, a warrant must first be served.

Note that where the district council is the culprit, you'll have to get a magistrates' order: the council can't issue a notice against itself.

Civil action

Taking a neighbour to the County Court under civil law allows you to get an injunction or court order restraining the neighbour from continuing the nuisance (in Scotland, you get an interdict). You might also be able to claim compensation.

However, a civil action can be expensive – consult a solicitor or your local Citizens Advice Bureau.

EXAMPLE: BARKING MAD

Which? reader Iain Mackintosh lives in a terraced house two doors away from a man who kept five Doberman dogs. Late at night, the dogs would begin to howl 'like wolves'. The owner said that two of the dogs were pregnant, which was why they were so noisy – small comfort to the Mackintosh household, whose sleep was broken night after night.

The local council was called in to investigate. They approached the owner and warned him that he would be taken to court unless the dogs could be kept quiet. The Mackintosh household was asked to keep noise diaries – a record of the date, time and duration of the barking, and to describe how the noise affected them (for example, if it woke them up at night). The council also offered to come out to record the noise level if it got bad again.

But after the owner was warned by the council that he could end up in court, the noise was greatly reduced. Perhaps the baby Dobermans arrived just in time.

Smells

District councils can investigate the nuisance caused by smells in the same way as for noise, and serve a notice on a smelly neighbour (with fines for ignoring it). Alternatively, you can take the neighbour to court yourself – though this can be expensive. The difficulty with proving smells nuisance is that it is even harder than with noise, as the following case study illustrates.

The nuisance of smells may be temporary (even if acute). And 'country smells' are hardly a nuisance in the country, where they would be quite unacceptable in town.

But nuisance is easier to prove where it is clear that the source of a smell could be relocated away from the vicinity. If the smell producer could take reasonable steps to remove smells, not to do so could be construed as creating a nuisance (for example, restaurants often use extractor systems and high chimneys to waft spicy odours away).

Where the smell is evidence of pollution or chemical hazard, you may be able to get quick action from agencies such as the National Rivers Authority or the Health and Safety Executive.

EXAMPLE: CLAMPDOWN ON SMELL

John and Yvonne Davis live in a farm cottage which backs on to a neighbouring farm's silage clamp (a grass heap which has been covered and allowed to rot – used for animal feed). The clamp gives off a foul smell as it matures during the autumn, and the Davises complained to the local council about the smell.

The council investigated and, after several visits by a council officer, agreed that the smell was a nuisance. They eventually served a notice on the owner telling him to clean up the area after he had earlier refused to re-site the clamp. But nothing happened, so the council took the owner to court.

In his defence, the owner argued that he had used the 'best practicable means' to find a proper location for the clamp (though it was only yards from the Davises' cottage). He also produced experts to show that the clamp was not defective in any way.

The magistrates decided to visit the site. By the time the case came to be heard – at least six months after the council notice – the smell was no longer very bad, and the case was dismissed.

Smoke

Much of urban Britain is given over to smokeless zones. Householders are not allowed to burn domestic fuels which produce smoke, nor can they light fires in their gardens which create smoke. If a neighbour persistently flouts these regulations, the district council Environmental Health Department should be called in.

Outside smokeless zones, householders are free to burn what they wish on their fires – inside or outside the house (though not hazardous substances). Persistent smoky bonfires might add up to a nuisance which the council could deal with, or you could take the culprit to court under civil law. You'd need records of the dates, times and nuisance caused, and preferably independent witnesses.

This – more than many other nuisances – may be inadvertent. A word with the offender may lead to some agreement that preserves good relations (for example, due warning of an occasional bonfire).

Trees

Trees can do damage well beyond the boundaries of their gardens – undermining your house by root action or falling on your house, shed or car. Branches falling off neighbours' trees can also damage your property.

In principle, you can take the owner to court for compensation for such damage (if the tree is in the street, you can take the council to court). But the owner is liable only for negligence – for failing to prevent such accidents if they were foreseeable. The owner would have a defence if the damage was not for want of action on his or her part, or was caused by natural action. So if the tree had been regularly pruned and pollarded, or the fall was caused by subsidence or storm, the owner might be in the clear. But it's no defence to say that the tree was there before your house or that it was wind-sown.

You have the right to cut the branches off a neighbour's tree where they cross the boundary of your property (they don't belong to you, though, so hand them back). And you can do the same with roots below the ground. These operations must be carried out from your side of the fence unless the owner gives permission for you to cross over. But remember that there are restrictions on what you can do to a tree covered by a Tree Preservation Order or in a conservation area – see p. 23.

Boundaries

Fences, hedges and walls between property can often be a source of dispute, especially over who is responsible for maintenance.

With a wall or fence, the ownership should be indicated in the title documents. There is no duty, however, to repair a fence or wall you own – only a possible liability if you don't. For example, if a crumbling wall collapses and injures a passer-by, that person could claim compensation from you. So maintaining walls and fences is prudent from this point of

113

view (if not also from a security point of view). Note that there are restrictions on the height of fences, walls and gates unless planning permission is given to exceed them – see p. 39.

If the boundary runs through a hedge, you and your neighbour are jointly responsible for it. Neither of you can reduce it in size or injure it without the other's agreement. With a hedge that is wholly on your side of the boundary (that is, planted on your side of a fence or wall), you can do as you please.

Access

Shared drives and paths can often lead to friction between neighbours, especially where there is no duty of maintenance in the title deeds of the house.

In some cases one of you owns the drive while the other has a right of way over it. In others the drive is divided up the middle: you each own half with right of way over the other half. Whichever the arrangement, the owner must not obstruct the person who has right of way. If there's no provision for maintenance of the drive, you'll have to agree on an arrangement.

═7═

OBJECTING TO A PLANNING APPLICATION

If your neighbour's plans require planning permission, you have the opportunity to oppose the application. To do this successfully you will have to act promptly and formulate your objection in the right way. If you are successful in stopping your neighbour from getting planning permission, he or she can appeal against refusal (or permission with unacceptable conditions). You can continue your opposition through the appeal.

Objecting to a planning application

The timetable for an objection

If a local planning authority notifies you of a planning application by a neighbour, there will normally be a 21-day deadline for registering any objections you have. This deadline runs from the date on the letter notifying you. With applications for listed buildings and conservation areas, you might get notification through press advertisements – again, with 21 days for a response.

The timetable may in practice be even tighter: although many authorities send letters to householders around a proposed development, this is not compulsory (outside Scotland, there is no requirement for the applicant to inform neighbours, except with some 'bad neighbour' developments – see p. 53). You might learn of an application only from press reports, a notice stuck up near the site, lists displayed in council buildings or libraries or just the local grapevine. By the time news reaches you of the application, the deadline for objections could be very close, so prompt action may be needed.

Of course, if you are lucky with your neighbours, the person applying for permission may inform you personally before putting in the application. This courtesy gives you the opportunity to discuss the proposals informally to see whether there is any cause for concern. If there are aspects of the application that you are unhappy about, raise them firmly and politely: your neighbour might be happy to amend it to accommodate you (and avoid turning you into an objector to the application). Even if you don't get everything you want, you may be able to reach an acceptable compromise without a full-blown battle over the planning application.

TIP

If you get wind of a planning application that could affect you, don't hang about. There may be very little time to register an objection, and, once planning permission is given, you cannot appeal against the decision. If necessary, register your opposition before you do everything necessary to mount a full-scale objection, so that the local planning authority doesn't treat it as an uncontested application. Ask the local planning authority for extra time to send in a fuller objection later. You can always withdraw your objection if you turn out to have got the wrong end of the stick.

Finding out more about the application

All planning applications are available to the public for inspection at the offices of the local planning authority. Use this right to read your neighbour's application and study any plans to see how it will affect you. Quote the reference number for the application which should be on any form of notification (though not knowing this is no obstacle to asking to see the application). Take pen and paper to make notes and

EXAMPLE: TOO LATE TO CHANGE THE PLANS

Sue Longley first learnt that her neighbour had got planning permission for an extension only when work began on it. She hadn't been notified of the application for planning permission: although the two houses were attached, there was no requirement for her to be informed.

If she had known about the application, Sue would have objected to it. There's a right of way around her neighbour's house to the back of her house – the new extension has made the path almost too narrow to get a bike through. And a window opens outwards on to the path which could injure a passer-by if opened suddenly.

---

drawings – details of the application will help you formulate your objection. If you cannot get to the planning offices, you can ask to be sent photocopies of the application and drawings (though this may be costly).

While you are at the planning offices, also ask to see the development plan for your area. The county structure plan will set out general principles for new development (see p. 160). If you're lucky, there will be an operative local plan which spells out in some detail how the local planning authority sees your area developing. A neighbour who wants to convert some rooms to offices in an area scheduled as residential is going to have an uphill struggle – and neighbours' objections could be crucial. On the other hand, your objections are less likely to be successful if the area is expected to remain mixed residential and commercial.

There will be a map of the area and a series of statements summarising the planning policies for it, plus notes, diagrams, illustrations and other explanatory detail. The plan may go down to details such as the number of houses per acre, the size of houses, and so on. Any such detail can help you with your objection – quoting an aspect of the development plan which conflicts with the planning application is probably the strongest card in your hand.

If you don't understand anything about the application or the development plan – technical details, for example – ask to speak to a planning officer. The staff are there to assist you.

TIP

Even if your neighbour consults you on a planning application, consider seeing the particulars for yourself at the local planning authority. It could be too late to oppose the application later if it turns out that your neighbour has been 'economical with the truth'. Even if your neighbour has laid out all the cards in front of you, it pays to study the plans at your leisure.

Formulating your objection

Even at this stage, it isn't too late to reason with your neighbour (especially if you have previously been on good terms). But unless the application is withdrawn or amended to meet your objections, you must now put your opposition into writing and submit it to the local planning authority. Your objection will be open for public inspection, just as the original application is. Note that a verbal objection in person to the planning officer or on the telephone is not acceptable – you must put pen to paper.

The nub of your objection must be a reason or reasons on planning grounds why the development should not be allowed. For example, you could seek to show that it is against the character of the area or not a form of development envisaged under the development plan. The development might put impossible strain on roads, sewerage or water supply systems. You might point out that amenities valued by the community (and the development plan) will be lost, that the development could intrude unacceptably on the countryside, or that there are already too many of whatever is planned in the area (guest-houses, shops or stables, say).

It will cut no ice to say that the development will harm your interests – that your life will be a misery or that the value of your home will fall. Important though these things are to you, they are irrelevant to the planning process. On the other hand, it is quite in order to say that the plan will destroy an amenity that you personally value, such as a piece of woodland or even a clear view of the road when driving your car out of your driveway. The key is to identify the public interest: your private concerns count only if they fit into the wider picture.

Try to formulate your objection clearly and without dramatic language. Don't be abusive – it won't help your case and may be actionable. Address the letter to the senior planning officer (Director of Planning or District Planning Officer), and head it with the planning reference number. If you can refer to the development plan, do so, and attach maps and plans if this will help your case. You could also submit photographs to demonstrate points you wish to highlight. The example on p. 120 indicates how such an objection might be written.

At the same time as you assemble your case, you should be talking to other neighbours affected by the proposals to get their support for opposing them – see p. 122. With most planning applications, this is the only chance for neighbours to have a say, so make full use of it.

TIP

Ask for a meeting with a planning officer at the local planning authority to discuss your neighbour's application. You can explain your worries and ask about anything you don't understand in the application and how it will be processed. The planning officer should be able to give you an idea of how likely the application is to succeed.

You can also ask who will take the decision: where there is controversy, it is likely to be a committee of councillors, which you can lobby.

---

15 Acacia Avenue
Slagthorpe
Borsetshire SP11 3DQ

23 September 1990

District Planning Officer
Slagthorpe District Council
Planning Department
Town Hall
Slagthorpe
Borsetshire SP10 1BR

Dear Sir

Planning Reference No: 940/13579/90
Application to build six small workshop units
on land behind 17 Acacia Avenue, Slagthorpe SP11 3DQ

I wish to enter my objection to the above planning application on the following grounds:

1. Acacia Avenue is an area scheduled under Policy H2 of the Slagthorpe District Plan for exclusively residential use, and is therefore unsuitable for this type of light industrial/office use. Considerable derelict land to the south of Slagthorpe is earmarked on the Borsetshire structure plan to be reclaimed for such industrial use.

2. As a narrow residential road less than 12 feet wide, Acacia Avenue does not have the capacity for the sort of traffic that would be created by staff at the units, lorry and van deliveries, refuse removal, etc.

3. The Slagthorpe Park estate on which Acacia Avenue forms a part is a uniquely well-preserved 1930s residential estate. Its integrity would be compromised by the type of prefabricated unit building envisaged.

4. The land behind 17 Acacia Avenue is crossed by a right of way, No P.23, which provides recreational amenity for residents of Acacia Avenue and adjoining roads.

5. A building of the height envisaged for these units on this position would dominate the gardens and houses of adjoining

houses – including ours – completely ruining the aspects which previously were of open land.

I hope that in view of these objections, planning permission will not be granted for this application in its present form. I should be grateful if my objection could be put before the Planning Committee. Please inform me of the outcome of this application.

Yours faithfully

Arthur Brown

Influencing the decision

Uncontentious decisions, particularly those which are unopposed, and routine decisions, for an advertising sign on a shop, say, are often taken by planning officers rather than the council planning committee. This is why it is important to make sure that a decision which is important to you is not unopposed.

With an application which looks likely to get serious consideration, go and see a local ward councillor (you'll get the address from the council offices or a library). If he or she is a member of the planning committee, you can put your case: if not, they will know councillors who are and may be persuaded to bend their ears. Your councillor may also be able to advise you on how the various members will be likely to vote – helpful in concentrating your fire. In some cases a planning application becomes a party political matter, and your councillor(s) is on what is for you the wrong side. You can always approach councillors for other areas or from another party to ask them for help.

Where the decision may be on a knife edge, you could write to the chairman of the planning committee setting out your case. You could even send a personal letter to each of the members of the planning committee. Make the letter concise and clear – councillors have more than enough paper to read.

You have the same rights as the applicant to attend council committee meetings and check that your case is heard (see p. 59). You don't have the right to address the committee, and permission for you to do so is unlikely to be given (though you could always ask if you can do so if the case is of great importance).

A public inquiry

With really contentious issues, the Secretary of State has the power to call in the application to decide it for himself. This almost invariably means a public inquiry at which the issues can be aired and witnesses cross-examined. If there's any danger that the local planning authority will give permission, and the issues are of national importance (encroachment on the Green Belt, for example), you could campaign for the Secretary of State to call in the application. The help of an MP is almost essential in this case – see p. 186 for how to approach MPS.

Getting support for your objection

If you are to be affected by a neighbour's plans for develop-ment, it is likely that others will too. Getting their support could help build up the weight to defeat the application (and, indeed, another neighbour might have a more powerful planning objection than you). Consider also the campaigning methods commonly used to defeat major planning applica-tions – letters to the press, publicity and celebrity support (more about these on p. 184).

Passing the word around

The first step is to alert those who will be affected by the development – they may be in the dark about it. You don't have to confine yourself to neighbours: people who work nearby or who use the amenities all have an interest. Getting a story in the local papers (or writing a letter) can help bring people together.

You can pass the word around informally with small developments, or by a round robin letter. With larger ones you could raise the issue through a local amenity group, residents' association, conservation group or other community bodies. If there isn't one in your area, perhaps now would be a good time to set one up (see p. 130 for how to go about this).

Co-ordinating objections

In an ideal world all objectors would write their own personal objections, each reflecting different aspects of their opposition to a development and all sticking carefully to planning issues. In practice it may take some organisation (and perhaps access to a word processor) to achieve this. While it might be tedious to have to badger other people and check up that they have done their bit, at least by co-ordinating the effort you can be sure that everyone has done what needs to be done.

If the proposal would affect more than half a dozen people, consider a petition of those affected.

Approach local organisations

If there is a local conservation group or amenity group, approach it for support. The local planning authority may give much more weight to their opposition than to that of individuals. And if the local conservation group doesn't appear to oppose a development, that may be seen as a factor in favour of the application.

If there is a third-tier council such as a parish council or town council (community council in Wales and Scotland), it will normally be sent details of all planning applications. Although this council has no official role in the planning decision, its views will be considered seriously. Its support could be vital – approach the chairman or convenor as soon as possible.

Finally, local branches of political parties should be approached (preferably by members) for support. Councillors may respond to their own party's views.

Get the support of official bodies

Many official bodies and quangos are consulted about planning applications – including the Nature Conservancy Council (where nature conservancy is involved), the Countryside Commission (with National Parks), the National Rivers Authority (for riverside development and development which might affect water or sewerage) and English Heritage and the Royal Fine Art Commission (for listed buildings). If you can persuade them to oppose an application, this will carry great weight, but you will need to encourage them gently unless the case has already achieved national publicity. The planning office should be able to tell you which ones have been consulted for the application you're interested in – but if you think they have an interest, you can approach those which aren't consulted.

An objection from the county council for a development that goes against the structure plan is also powerful. Similarly, the highways authority should be encouraged to object if the development will have an impact on roads.

National conservation groups

The support of national groups such as the Civic Trust, the Council for the Protection of Rural England and the Ramblers' Association can help in defeating a planning application. You may also get some helpful advice and encouragement from them, drawing on their experience of similar battles elsewhere. Some major organisations are listed in Sources of Help (see pp. 199 to 202).

Make an impact with your objection

It's important to remember that this may be the only opportunity to enter objections to a planning application. Objectors can't appeal if the decision is in favour of the application, so your aim must be to get a 'no' decision.

For what happens to the planning application as it goes through to the point of decision, see p. 57. If the decision goes against the application, your neighbour can appeal to the Secretary of State, and you can again raise your objections – see p. 126.

Note that if you feel that the local planning authority has not handled the decision-making process properly, you can raise it with the Local Ombudsman (see p. 63).

EXAMPLE: DEFENDING THE BROADS

Avril and Hugh Rodway live in a quiet country lane opposite a small holiday camp of chalets and houseboats in East Anglia. In August 1989 they received a letter informing them that new owners of the camp had applied for planning permission to build 70 houses, which would have attracted full-time residents rather than summer holiday-makers. The estate would have incorporated adjoining woodland, and put extra pressure on the river.

With only a few days left to put in objections, the Rodways alerted as many people as possible (the notice had been sent to only four houses in their lane). They put together a petition which attracted 50 signatures – a lot for a sparsely populated area. And they started lobbying their town council.

Their objection pointed out that the plans were an inappropriate overdevelopment of the site, that the lanes were unsuitable for such an increase in traffic and that there would be harm to wildlife (the woods are breeding grounds for the rare swallow-tailed butterfly). The town council agreed unanimously to oppose the application, and the Norfolk Society added its support.

125

Every member of the district council planning committee was sent a letter outlining the objections, and the Rodways made sure that their own very helpful councillor was well briefed. When it came to the final decision, the developer withdrew the application (it was by now October).

With very few people on the ground, the campaign ran itself informally, rather than by having meetings or committees. Avril found her word processor invaluable, and was able to use her fax as a photocopier. The Rodways recommend leaving no stone unturned – and warn that campaigners can expect to put in a lot of time over a fairly short period.

Fighting an appeal

A neighbour who is refused planning permission, or granted it subject to unacceptable conditions, has a right of appeal to the Secretary of State. This can be a written appeal (based on exchange of papers), a local inquiry at which evidence is heard and witnesses cross-examined or an informal hearing – in each case, presided over by an independent inspector (see Chapter 4).

You will have the opportunity to state your views as part of the appeals process, whether or not you have objected to the planning application in the first place. As neighbours affected by the development, you will be in the group known as 'interested persons' or third parties.

Making further representations

If you have objected to the planning application, your original objections will be submitted to the appeal by the local planning authority as part of its submission. You will also be informed of the appeal by the local planning authority, with 21 days to elaborate or make further comments. You can inspect the grounds of appeal lodged by your neighbour at the local planning authority offices, and it is worth putting in further submissions if there are points that you wish to reply to.

If you haven't already objected, it's not too late to act: you can still put in comments – though you won't normally be invited to do so. The local planning authority will put up notices advertising the appeal around the site and elsewhere, and you can write in with your representation by a set date.

Whichever category you fall into, follow the same rules as for an objection (see above). Stick to planning points, be clear and logical and muster support from neighbours.

The site visit

The appeal inspector will make a visit to the site at some stage, which you can ask to attend. However, the inspector won't discuss the merits of the appeal during the site visit, with you, the appellant or the local planning authority. Unless you are concerned that some matter of fact would be overlooked on a site visit, it may not be necessary to turn up (see p. 77).

Giving evidence at a public inquiry

With public inquiries (see p. 81), you can ask for the opportunity to put your point of view in evidence: the neighbour who is appealing can question you (and in some cases you may be able to question him or her).

The weight of public opposition should not be a factor in deciding the appeal, so you shouldn't use these rights to a hearing merely to pile in more and more opposition. But if what you regard as key planning arguments are not getting a fair exposure, then use these rights to state them. And make sure that the inspector is aware of the extent of public opposition.

> **TIP**
>
> In a case that is important to you, consider at least taking the advice of a consultant town planner – even if it's only for a discussion of the issues after a glance through the papers. An objective view could save you time and effort – and perhaps help you choose a winning strategy that had not occurred to you.

Costs

The inspector can award costs against the person appealing or the local planning authority in certain circumstances (see p. 84). But the costs of third parties are almost never awarded against a loser, so you'll have to bear the costs of your opposition yourself.

Getting professional assistance

You don't need professional representation to oppose a planning application, or to take part in an appeal, even if there is to be a public inquiry. But with complicated cases – or if you prefer not to deal with such matters yourself – you can appoint someone else to act for you. It doesn't have to be an expert; you could ask a friend with a bent for administrative matters. But most people seeking help will want to use a professional with knowledge of the planning system.

The developer will often have the expertise of an architect (and large developers can call on lawyers and planning professionals). If you can afford the cost, you could employ a consultant chartered town planner (lists for your area are available from the Royal Town Planning Institute – address on p. 198). Other types of consultants may be able to offer expert advice, particularly on environmental issues such as wildlife impact and pollution. Payment is likely to be based on the time you take up and is unlikely to be less than £30 an hour (ask for an estimate in advance).

If employing a consultant is beyond your means, there are various planning advice services up and down the country which can assist. Your local Citizens Advice Bureau may also be able to advise. Voluntary bodies will certainly give advice, but do not expect them to back you beyond that, except in cases of great injustice or public interest.

EXAMPLE: AVERSION TO CONVERSION

Mrs Wallis lives in a conservation area in a Grade II listed building. Next door is an eighteenth-century cottage, also listed, whose owner applied for planning permission to construct a separate two-storey building in the garden. Mrs Wallis and the local amenity society objected to this on the grounds of overdevelopment, and they were delighted when the planning committee agreed.

The neighbour appealed, and Mrs Wallis took the opportunity to restate her objections. Unfortunately, the neighbour won the appeal: the then Secretary of State had expressed support for 'infilling' of sites.

In the end the neighbour sold the house without carrying out the work. The new owner approached Mrs Wallis about building a single-storey extension which was much more acceptable – she even wrote to the planners saying so. Mrs Wallis feels that the extension protects the cottage from further development, even though the character of the cottage has been irrevocably altered.

=== 8 ===

IMPROVING YOUR NEIGHBOURHOOD

Even if your neighbours aren't hoping to open an all-night hamburger bar next door, there will be aspects of your area that you would like to see improved. People may be using quiet residential areas to run businesses or ruining the rural peace by staging motocross events in a nearby field. Run-down houses, wrecked cars, uneven pavements, derelict land, dog mess, graffiti, rush-hour traffic in residential streets – all of these can spoil your immediate environment.

A first step towards improving your neighbourhood is to consider joining forces with your neighbours in a residents' or local amenity group – you are much more likely to succeed if you are not just an isolated individual.

Joining forces

Many of the things that you might want to do to improve your area require the help of other people and bodies. For example, your local council may have the powers needed to make some real changes in your neighbourhood. Or an injection of cash from a charity or other grant-making body could help get a project off the ground. Local radio stations and newspapers may be able to publicise your plans and get people backing your aims. In some cases you may need the assistance of a Member of Parliament (or even a Member of the European Parliament). You are much more likely to get such people and bodies on your side if you join forces with others to set up some sort of community group which can speak for your area on these matters.

And cash for environmental schemes is tight these days: there's no doubt that organised groups stand a better chance of getting the help and support they need. If you are a representative group, you can be more ambitious than individuals about the schemes you want to see. Further, the emphasis now is very much on partnership between public bodies (like councils) and voluntary groups: you may achieve more, faster, if you band together and show that as a community you can raise funds of your own and do some of the work yourself.

There may already be a suitable community organisation to work through (even if it is moribund, it will at least have a name and some members to start from). If there isn't, you can set one up. An *ad hoc* group is one option, to pursue a particular issue (preventing the use of your road as a traffic rat-run, for example). Once the battle is over, the group can cease to exist. Of you could set up a more permanent residents' association or local amenity group which looks at all the issues affecting your neighbourhood. Note that you might have to do both on occasions: for example, a residents' association covering several streets might not be keen to take up a traffic issue relating to one particular street if there's any chance that the problem would be shifted into neighbouring streets.

Setting up a community group

You can set up a community group without any paperwork, formal structure, elected officers and the rest – and for a one-off campaign this could be quite sufficient. But for a group which you expect to continue for any length of time, or which will need to raise some funds from supporters, it makes sense to set it up formally with members (and supporters), officers, a bank account, etc. Apart from helping it to continue if individuals move out of the area or drop out, a proper structure can help resolve differences which may arise in any organisation.

Here are some of the things to think about in setting up a group:

- define the aims of the group. Try to keep it well focused, so that the organisation doesn't get diverted into fringe issues, and positive, so that it's not just 'against' something but 'for' improving the area
- raise some funds to cover costs, of circulars or leaflets, for example. A small subscription with the odd fund-raising draw can provide the cash to keep a small group ticking over (see p. 133).
- manage the funds. Appoint a treasurer, open a bank or building society account, draw up simple accounts showing money paid in and out, and what the amounts are being spent on, and have another member audit the books
- appoint other officers. A secretary to deal with correspondence and a chairman or chairwoman to chair meetings and act as a figurehead are a minimum
- print your own stationery – an attractive letterhead gives a group credibility and may help your letters get noticed
- communications. A simple newsletter on two sides of A4 and hand-delivered can disseminate information and build up support (a member with a home computer may be able to make this look very professional)
- publicity. The odd press release to the local newspapers (or even a telephone call) can get coverage, even if it's only of the founding meeting or the annual meeting
- formal membership, with a subscription and a membership card giving the holder the right to vote at meetings (again, a member with a home computer can probably take care of this and produce sticky labels easily)
- campaigns. Collect signatures on petitions, hold public meetings, write letters to the press, lobby councillors and

---

TIP

Form a steering group or committee at an early stage: people are much more impressed by a group than an individual who may just appear to have a bee in the bonnet about something.

MPS, leaflet the general public, stage publicity-catching stunts, and so on (see p. 184).

Spread the work around by having a membership secretary, campaigns officer, publicity officer, and so on.

A successful group usually depends on a nucleus of four to six people who can always be relied upon to turn up for meetings, events, and so on. This avoids one person doing all the work and means that the group is more likely to survive when a key person moves on. Equally, when there are no major issues on the agenda, active support may fall away: local groups which recognise this likelihood will survive until they are needed again if they accept a period of dormancy and minimal output.

TIP

Invite a local councillor to join your group. He or she will be able to give you helpful advice, to liaise with the council and probably raise your profile.

Raising funds for local groups

There are sources of money for local and community groups, though demand for funds is high and there is never enough to satisfy all possible claims. A group which approaches others for funds will normally have to show that it is raising money through its own efforts.

No two fund-raising efforts are the same, but try to use the skills and enthusiasm of your members to choose methods which will help your aims. Fund-raising can draw in supporters, advertise your cause, get publicity and even help achieve your objectives (a sponsored litter-picking competition in the local park, for example). Raffles, hundred clubs, draws, socials and dances, sponsored walks/swims/aerobics, collecting recyclable materials, market stalls, car boot sales – the list is endless.

TIP

If there's a celebrity in the area, consider inviting him or her to join the committee, even if it's only as a sort of figurehead president. This will improve the credibility of your group, attract publicity and help in campaigning (see p. 184 for more about using celebrities).

Note that fund-raising raffles and lotteries may need a gaming licence if the prizes are not drawn at the time the tickets are sold – further details from your local council.

Sources of finance

Sources of Help (see p. 205) includes details of some publications that might help give you ideas for raising larger sums of money. Options worth considering include:

- the local council. It may have a budget to support voluntary groups, or be able to suggest sources of funding. It may even have someone who liaises with local voluntary groups which can help
- local businesses – especially if you can show that it would help their business and/or give them some recognition by way of publicity
- landowners and landlords – improvements could help raise the value of their land or property (and many large landowners are charitable trusts)
- charities. Realistically, it's worth approaching only charities with local links or an interest in the project unless it's a case of national importance
- national voluntary organisations – for example, if funds are needed to make a bird sanctuary, contact the Royal Society for the Protection of Birds
- large companies with social programmes – though, again, it's probable that they'll fund projects only in areas in which they have plant or buildings

- national bodies – Business in the Community, for example, or the various church social organisations (approach local churches for these).

There are various guides and directories for national grant-making trusts (see p. 205). But your local Council for Voluntary Services may also produce a list of local sources – contact it through your local council. The Civic Trust (address on p. 199) has details of many sources of funds, though you may do better with local fund-raising initially.

TIP

If you are raising money for a particular project (restoring a building, say), setting up a trust may help in getting funds – especially if it can be charitable. This allows donors to claim tax relief on gifts (and if they take out covenants for regular gifts, this can add up to £7 to every £10 they hand over). It also makes it easier to get money from other charities. Legal advice is essential in setting up a trust, but some publications on the merits of setting up a charity are listed on p. 204.

Breaches of planning regulations

Every building and every site has a defined use under planning law – and it can't be changed without planning permission. Apart from decorating, internal alterations and minor external works, most buildings cannot be developed without planning permission (see Chapter 1). Listed buildings and buildings in conservation and other special areas are governed by even stricter rules (see Chapter 5).

Often, the planning rules are broken unintentionally, through ignorance or error. In many cases, though, people break the planning regulations because they think they won't be found out. And in some cases people who have been refused planning permission go ahead anyway or ignore the conditions made when planning permission was granted.

Local planning authorities employ enforcement officers to crack down on such activities. In response to tip-offs from local amenity groups, the public or council staff – or just by touring their areas – they identify potential breaches of the regulations. A visit to the site follows so that the enforcement officer can find out what's happening and tell the developer what action has to be taken.

The local planning authority will normally bend over backwards to help sort out the problem. For example, a householder who has failed to apply for the necessary planning permission will be urged to submit an application very quickly (unless what he or she is up to is so clearly unacceptable that doing so will be a waste of time). The local planning authority will probably suggest that work stops pending planning permission.

With a breach of conditions or where someone refused planning permission has gone ahead anyway, the local planning authority will want a firm commitment to observe the regulations. If this is not given (or given but not observed), then the local planning authority can wheel out its enforcement powers.

Enforcement notices

The local planning authority's chief weapon is the enforcement notice, which forces the developer to abide by the planning rules. If necessary, the enforcement notice can demand that work already done be reversed or that a building which has not had planning permission be demolished. In most cases the environment notice is effective only if it is issued within four years of the development taking place.

The enforcement notice must be sent to the developer, with the following information:

- what planning regulations have been breached (these must be specified exactly and correctly)
- the action the local planning authority requires to restore the site (this could include demolishing whatever has been built on it)

- the time-limit for carrying out this action – this cannot be fewer than 28 days after the date the enforcement notice is issued to everyone who has to get one (see below)
- the date on which the notice is issued
- why the local planning authority has resorted to issuing an enforcement notice
- the exact site covered by the notice.

Copies of the notice must be sent to any other owners of the land (in the widest sense – see p. 50), to occupiers of the land (that is, tenants and licensees) and to anyone else with a material interest, all within 28 days of the date the notice was issued. In most cases the offender either complies with the enforcement notice or opens negotiations with the local planning authority to find a compromise. The developer has the option of appealing against the enforcement notice – see below for details. If he or she ignores it the recalcitrant developer may be fined. The local planning authority can, as a last resort, itself take action to restore the site.

Certain breaches of planning rules may be so unacceptable as to need to be brought to an immediate halt. Once an enforcement notice has been issued, a stop notice may be served in certain circumstances to halt the activity (for example, repairing cars from a workshop on a residential estate).

Appeals against an enforcement notice

Anyone served with an enforcement notice can appeal against it to the Secretary of State. In practice the appeal will normally be decided by an inspector, as with planning appeals (see p. 66). The person appealing has a choice between a written appeal and a public inquiry, though the Secretary of State can insist on a public inquiry.

The appeal has to be made before the date on which the notice has to be carried out. Once the appeal is lodged, the enforcement notice is suspended pending the appeal (though a stop notice remains in force). An appeal can be made only on one of the following grounds:

- planning permission ought to be given for the development (effectively similar to an appeal against refusal of planning permission – see p. 69)
- the details in the enforcement notice are not a breach of planning regulations
- the breach of planning regulations in the notice has not actually taken place
- the development took place more than four years earlier (for types covered by the four-year rule) or before 1964 (when time-limits applied to all developments)
- the enforcement notice was not properly served on everyone who should have received one
- the steps required to rectify the situation are excessive
- the time-limit for the rectification is unreasonably short (success with this ground for an appeal would only delay the action).

Interested parties such as neighbours and local groups will be invited to make submissions to the appeal. They can inspect the grounds for appeal and the local planning authority's case, and ask to be present on the site visit. And if there is a local inquiry, such people and organisations can give evidence and perhaps question the person appealing. The procedures are much the same as for planning appeals – see p. 72.

If you're appealing against an enforcement notice

The aim should be always to avoid finding yourself appealing against an enforcement notice. You might find yourself in an enforcement officer's firing-line because you had never applied for or received the necessary planning permission for an extension, a change of use, or even some minor alteration to a building in a conservation area. But it should be possible to get the planning permission you need – or tailor your plans to get it – without running up against an enforcement notice. If you cannot get the planning permission to let you go ahead, you can follow the appeals procedure (see Chapter 4).

But you might have to appeal against an enforcement notice if the local planning authority serves one immediately – because it judges the damage to the local environment to be such as not to allow the delay of applying for planning permission. In these circumstances take advice from a solicitor or a planning consultant. There's a useful booklet on the process from the Planning Inspectorate called *Enforcement Notice Appeals: A Guide to Procedure* (see p. 195 for addresses to write to).

Ways to improve your neighbourhood

What follows is a brief run-down of some common environmental problems, together with details of which agencies have powers to deal with them.

One word of warning, though: don't expect 100 per cent success. As with other planning issues, the outcome of some environmental disputes often satisfies none of the parties completely. Most activity has to go on in someone's back yard: the aim is to find the 'least worst solution' which ensures that the total disruption to the community is minimised and that no individual bears the whole brunt.

Traffic

If you are concerned about heavy traffic in your area, take it up with the local highway authority. This is usually the county council, but the district councils have responsibility for footpaths, bridleways and urban roads which are neither trunk roads nor classified. Note that local councils don't have control over trunk roads and other special roads like motorways – these are the responsibility of the Secretary of State for Transport.

What you can get done about traffic problems will depend on how your road is seen by the local highway authority. The authority will not, for example, be prepared to do much to deter traffic from using a main road – or even a minor road

---

TIP

Collect data to back your case for action on traffic. Over a typical period (the rush hour, a day, a week) carry out a traffic count, listing cars, vans, buses, lorries, etc. separately. If there are peaks and troughs, split the count into sections (hours, half-hours or whatever). The following information might be useful in particular cases:

- details of destinations of traffic (you may be able to see this with lorries and vans – or ask drivers while they are stopped at lights)
- lists of accidents or crashes, including dates, time, weather conditions, type of vehicle and details of any personal injuries
- estimates of speeds and noise levels.

It's unlikely that the local authority will take action without doing its own survey (it can install equipment to measure volume and speed cheaply and easily) – but your figures could help convince them of the need for a survey.

---

which is clearly the main route between two points – except as part of a major scheme to build a new trunk road or by-pass. Local authorities are also reluctant to take steps in one area that would simply displace traffic into other equally unsuitable areas.

But if your quiet residential road is being used as a rush-hour rat-run or a short cut for heavy lorries, you may be able to persuade your local authority to act. The options include road closures, 'traffic management schemes' to make it difficult for traffic to find a way through the area, and measures such as bollards and road narrowing to keep lorries out. Lorries can be banned at night unless they get permits to make necessary deliveries, and parking restrictions can be applied for heavy goods vehicles.

And even where you can't persuade the local authority to eradicate traffic, the authority can take steps to reduce the danger of fast-moving traffic. 'Traffic-calming measures', such as 'sleeping policemen' (humps in the road) and narrow pinch-points, can slow traffic down. On major roads, barriers can protect pedestrians from the traffic, with special crash barriers on dangerous corners. And there should be sufficient pedestrian crossing points (with additional help on crossings near schools from lollipop men and women).

EXAMPLE: STEMMING THE FLOW IN NEW CROSS

The residents of Gellatly Road in south-east London became concerned at the consistent volume of commuter traffic using their residential road as a short cut. The noise continued late into the night, and speeds were alarming, especially in the downhill direction. After several accidents involving damage to property and injuries to people, they decided to campaign to close the road to through traffic.

They persuaded the council to survey the traffic. This showed that more than 16,000 vehicles a day were using the road. Average speeds were also high: well over 30mph despite the speed-limit (and much higher at off-peak times). A petition attracted the signatures of almost all the residents, and posters were put up highlighting the problem and demanding closure. The residents lobbied the borough council for action, enlisting the support of their local councillors and MP. And they staged a demonstration which stopped traffic in the early-morning rush-hour (with police co-operation) – this brought a lot of publicity.

The council felt unable to close the road, since this would shift the traffic on to neighbouring residential roads. But it agreed to alter the priority at a junction at the top of the hill and to introduce measures to slow traffic down. The pavements are to be extended towards the centre of the road in several places, to provide protection for parked cars. And 'sleeping policemen' are to be installed to keep speeds down (when resources are available).

141

Parking

The growth in car ownership means that many urban residential roads are choked with parked cars. And if you live near a station or commercial centre, you may find parking outside your home difficult during the day.

There's no right to park your car outside your home (or anywhere else, for that matter). Putting hard standing in front of your house will need planning permission if it creates a new way on to a trunk or classified road (as well as council permission to lower the kerb). Even then, there's always the danger that someone will park across the exit.

If parking by non-residents is becoming a problem in your area, you might consider asking the council to introduce a residents' parking scheme. This restricts parking to people who display a local resident's parking permit, which they usually have to renew each year. As part of setting up such a scheme, the council may also review off-street parking provision (for example, for offices nearby). And yellow lines are likely to be drawn along the sides of the road demarcating areas available for parking – this may discourage people from blocking your drive or hard standing.

Residents' parking schemes will not solve all parking problems, however. The council won't restrict the number of permits it issues to the number of places available – so you may still not be able to park near your home. And there'll be a yearly charge for a permit.

If parking space is getting short in your area, make sure the council takes this into account in considering planning applications. For example, if someone applies for permission to build a small block of flats, the developer could be required to include off-street parking as part of the development. The same would apply if a developer wanted to divide a large house into flats.

Dereliction

If a run-down house or piece of derelict land spoils your neighbourhood, draw it to the attention of your district council. The council has powers to make the owners maintain land and buildings.

Waste ground is often a problem, with illegal dumping and any walls covered in graffiti. If the council won't or can't act, this is a prime candidate for local action: many waste-land sites have been converted into community gardens, or paved and provided with benches where people can sit. Creepers and trees can screen ugly walls.

If your area is particularly run down, consider asking the council to designate it for priority treatment – funds may be available from special government programmes (especially in inner-city areas).

EXAMPLE: CLEAN WORK AT THE CROSSROADS

Newport and District Civic Society in Shropshire obtained permission from the local council to beautify a neglected area of land beside a crossroads in Newport. The site was edged in paving slabs with a border of old setts. Forsythia, a rowan tree, rambling roses and various shrubs were planted and a temporary fence put around the perimeter to protect the young plants. The whole exercise cost around £120.

Recreational amenities

Derelict land in the country can be converted into parks, nature reserves, play areas and community forests. Apart from smartening up tatty or poorly used plots, this would head off developers who could choose such eyesores to locate new developments.

The Countryside Commission encourages local authorities to set up country parks and community forests – approach your local council for details. Smaller-scale projects, such as nature reserves and play areas, can be carried out by local groups. One of the network of Groundwork Trusts may be able to help with the assistance of business sponsorship (see p. 202 for the address of Groundwork Foundation).

Dumping and rubbish in the streets

Councils have considerable powers to stop dumping of waste, old cars and rubbish (and recent legislation gives them stronger powers to deal with 'fly-tipping' – the dumping of building waste in streets). They are to get stronger powers to clean up litter (see below). The problem is often a lack of staff to enforce the powers.

If your area is strewn with abandoned cars, old bedspreads and other rubbish, a concerted effort by local residents to lobby the local council could be the best way of stopping it. The first step is to get local support for a clean-up: leaflet every house. Then make sure that everyone knows how to get rid of waste at council dumps or recycling centres. Get the council Environmental Health Department to remove existing waste and abandoned cars. At the same time, waste or derelict land used for dumping needs to be cleared (see above). A period of vigilance by council staff and residents to stop the dumping building up will help ensure that there is no slipping back.

Litter

Councils are being encouraged by Parliament to do more about litter in the streets and public places, with new powers in the Environmental Protection Act 1990:

- Landowners can be fined if they do not maintain adequate standards, whether in a shopping precinct, car-park or recreation ground.
- Local authorities can be taken to court if they do not keep the streets and other public places clean.

- The penalties for dropping litter have been raised, with spot fines of £10 for dropping litter.

The Act defines four levels of cleanliness, from Grade A (no litter or refuse) through to Grade D (badly littered). Grade B is litter-free apart from odd items like cigarette stubs; Grade C has lots of smaller bits of litter, such as fast-food packaging. Every local authority must divide its area into seven zones, according to the standards of cleanliness which will be permitted. Category 1 zones, for example, cover town centres: they must be kept up to Grade A – any lapse into Grade B must be restored within six hours. Category 7 zones have up to *two weeks* to be left at Grade C before returning to Grade A – and so on.

The Act will enable you to take the local authority to court if it does not keep your area up to scratch. You can also take other bodies and organisations to court if they fail to keep their land up to the mark (landowners, garages, housing associations, and so on). If they don't comply with a litter abatement order, there'll be fines.

Dog mess

An increasing number of councils have by-laws to deal with dog mess in streets, parks and public places. Dog-owners can be fined if their dogs foul streets, parks, playgrounds and other public places (rarely enforced). Dogs can be banned from certain recreational areas (including beaches), while other areas can be designated dog-exercising areas, with perhaps small areas of sand provided for dog toilets.

Recognising that there will always be irresponsible owners, some councils are setting up dog warden schemes, and some urban councils provide special equipment for cleaning up dog mess ('pooper scoopers'). If there is a problem with dog mess or strays in your area, these are all options to be explored with the council.

145

Noise in the streets

Remedies against noisy neighbours are discussed in Chapter 6, but there are restrictions on noise in public places which are often not enforced.

For example, ice-cream vans should not operate their loudspeakers outside the hours of noon to 7pm. The same applies to mobile butchers, bakers, and so on.

And it's illegal to sound a car horn while the car is stationary, or while moving between 11.30pm and 7am in a built-up area (unless there's a danger to another moving vehicle). However, prosecutions are rare.

Local authority by-laws often apply to noise in public places, such as parks, beaches and shopping centres. Check with your council Environmental Health Department.

Other improvements to the neighbourhood

There is no end to the improvements that can be made to community life by a determined amenity group, and other steps to improve the quality of life in your area include:

- better street lighting, to deter street crime and improve safety – approach your district council
- a neighbourhood watch scheme – the local police station can advise
- tree-planting (and protection)
- home insulation schemes – especially for the elderly and disabled
- facilities for pre-school children.

Preserving the character of the neighbourhood

If your neighbourhood is of special architectural or historic interest, one way of preserving its character and improving it is to have it declared a conservation area. Even if your area can't become a conservation area, you may be able to stop unsuitable development by preserving individual buildings through listing – see p. 149. And you can help preserve the trees in your area by use of Tree Preservation Orders – see p. 151.

There are useful circulars from the three Secretaries of State about listed buildings and conservation areas; these are available from HMSO Books (address on p. 196).

Conservation areas

Conservation areas have a special architectural or historic character which it is desirable to preserve or enhance. District councils are under an obligation to assess which parts of their territory might qualify, and to designate them as conservation areas. County councils may also designate conservation areas in consultation with the district council. In London, English Heritage can designate a conservation area in consultation with the borough council and with the permission of the Secretary of State.

The planning regulations are much stricter in conservation areas (for details, see p. 96):

- some work which would affect the external appearance of buildings requires planning permission. This includes stone cladding
- trees cannot be felled, topped, lopped or wilfully damaged without notice (see p. 151)
- although you can still build small extensions or outbuildings without planning permission, the limits on size, etc. are tighter
- loft and roof extensions always need planning permission
- demolition requires special conservation area consent (see p. 97).

In addition, the local planning authority often takes out 'Article 4' powers (see p. 98), which restrict external work even further. For example, it can specify that reroofing has to be in slate, doors and windows can be replaced only in the same style and materials, and repainting may have to be done in specific colours.

The procedure for creating a conservation area is simple: the planning authority resolves to do it and publishes various official notices; there is no appeal against the decision. The main constraint is that designating a conservation area creates work for the local planning authority. Extra staff will be needed to deal with the increase in planning work; planning applications need extra publicising; and a conservation area plan must be drawn up.

The conservation area plan sets out how the character and appearance of the area will be preserved and enhanced, usually a combination of listing buildings, restricting some types of development and eliminating activities out of character with the tone of the area. The draft must be published and submitted for discussion at a public meeting in the area. The final plan must take account of views expressed at that meeting.

TIP

If you want your neighbourhood designated a conservation area, you will have to persuade your local council that it is of special architectural or historic interest. Even if the council has decided against declaring the neighbourhood a conservation area in the past, it has a duty to review such decisions from time to time (you could press for a review when the local plan is being drawn up or reviewed – see p. 164). And if the district council is unsympathetic, you could lobby the county council (or even the Secretary of State).

The support of national conservation societies (addresses on pp. 199–200) and architects will help demonstrate architectural interest. Research, together with the assistance of older residents and any local history society, can establish historic interest. Even if no single building is of merit, an area may still qualify because of the group value (whole streets, layout, amenities, etc.).

Preserving buildings of merit

If an area isn't a conservation area, there's nothing to stop a developer demolishing buildings in it unless they have been listed as of special architectural or historic interest. You'll find more about listed buildings in Chapter 5, but it's worth noting that anyone can nominate a building for listing (you don't have to be the owner).

Once listed, a building can be demolished only with listed building consent, which requires a similar process to applying for planning permission. This gives people the opportunity to oppose whatever it is that the developer wants to do. And local planning authorities are required to take extra care to preserve the setting of listed buildings when considering planning applications on nearby buildings.

The local planning authority will have a form for nominating a building to be listed. If the building is under threat of demolition or radical alteration, you can ask the local planning authority to put a building preservation notice on it. This means that the building must be treated as listed for six months, giving time for the listing process to be completed.

If a listed building is falling into disrepair, the local planning authority can take steps to repair it, or even compulsorily purchase it.

TIP

Having a building listed means proving special historic or architectural interest. As with a conservation area, to demonstrate the building is of architectural interest, seek the support of national conservation groups and architects (especially those associated with the period or style of the building). Research at a library or among older inhabitants or with the help of the local history society may prove that the building is of historic interest.

149

EXAMPLE: LIST IT YOURSELF

Brentwood Civic Society became concerned in the 1970s about the loss of historical buildings in the town. The society asked the Department of the Environment to update the list of listed buildings, but the Department said it did not have the resources to do so. The society surveyed all the historic buildings in the town and submitted its findings to both the Department of the Environment and Essex County Council. An updated list was quickly prepared with the new additions.

EXAMPLE: REBUILDING AN ITALIANATE DREAM IN CAMBERWELL

Denmark Hill Station was built in 1866, straddling a railway cutting in Camberwell. A two-storey central pavilion flanked by Italianate domed roofs, it was described by the architectural correspondent of *The Times* as 'a vintage Tuscan palazzo'. But after it was burnt out in a fire in 1980, it became clear that British Rail could not afford to restore it. A small prefabricated station building looked to be inevitable, in an area of Victorian buildings.

The Camberwell Society launched an appeal, raising just over £4000. This drew in the Southwark Environment Trust, and British Rail agreed to match the funds £ for £ from its own Environment Fund. Local celebrities joined the battle, and national figures, such as Marcus Binney of SAVE and Sir John Betjeman, added their weight.

Substantial funds came from the Historic Buildings Council and the Greater London Council, doubled by British Rail to produce almost £200,000. But the clinching investment came from brewer David Bruce, who agreed to convert the central pavilion into a pub with real ale brewed on the premises. The aptly named Phoenix and Firkin is now a popular and unique drinking place, in Italianate surroundings above the railway lines.

Tree Preservation Orders

Trees are automatically protected from destruction or mutilation in a conservation area, but other trees can be protected by means of a Tree Preservation Order (TPO). It might be foolish to seek to put Tree Preservation Orders on every tree in your area, especially where you live in the country, but very old trees or those that are a unique feature of the landscape – or ones which are known to be under threat – should be protected by orders.

Once covered by an order, a tree cannot be felled without the consent of the local planning authority. Nor can it be lopped or pollarded without permission (lopping is chopping off branches with anything bigger than secateurs). And the tree must not be uprooted (by adjacent building works, for example), wilfully damaged (by hooliganism, say) or wilfully destroyed. The latter can include destruction by negligence (for example, damaging the roots while working nearby) or by intention (poisoning it, say).

The only exception to these extensive protective restrictions applies to a tree which is dangerous, dying or dead. A tree covered by an order can be felled if it is leaning dangerously after a gale, for example (though it might have to be replaced with a similar tree). Where woodland is covered, normal forestry operations may be allowed by the Tree Preservation Order so long as replacement trees are planted.

A Tree Preservation Order is normally made by the district council, which has a duty to preserve trees and also to plant them where appropriate. But county councils can also make TPOs in certain circumstances – where they are giving the

---

TIP

If a much-loved tree is threatened which isn't covered by a Tree Preservation Order, get a provisional Tree Preservation Order issued. This stops it being felled for up to six months while a full order is made.

---

planning permission, for example, or where the land is covered by more than one district council. An order can be made for a single tree, a group of trees or woodland as a whole. Hedgerows cannot be covered, although trees in a hedgerow can.

PART 3

Conserving Your Environment

BRITAIN'S PLANNING SYSTEM

Most of the development discussed so far has been local and small-scale – an extension to a house or permission to build a few houses, for example. But what happens if someone has plans which could totally change the whole area in which you live? How can you defend your local environment against proposals to drive a motorway through it, or site a shopping centre nearby, or build a new village on open land?

Much of what has already been written in earlier chapters about the planning system and how to campaign within it applies equally in these cases. But the scale of the process is much greater, since you may be facing large corporations or even central government itself. This scale should not deter you, however: in all the cases examined, local people were able to either completely stop proposals affecting their area or change them substantially to avoid some of the worst consequences.

How Britain's planning system works

Planning in Great Britain is administered at two levels: central government influences the process through the Secretary of State, who is at the apex of the system, and local planning authorities at county/region and district level administer it from day to day. The framework that governs the system is the Town and Country Planning Act 1971 (or the equivalent in Scotland – see p. 10), but in each area strategic and local development plans provide the yardstick by which planning decisions are judged.

The Secretary of State

At government level, planning is the responsibility of the Secretary of State: in England the Secretary of State for the Environment, in Wales the Secretary of State for Wales, and in Scotland the Secretary of State for Scotland.

Some other ministers may make what are effectively planning decisions:

- motorways and trunk roads are controlled by the Secretary of State for Transport
- the Secretary of State for Trade and Industry has powers (not much used now) to locate industrial development
- the Minister of Agriculture, Fisheries and Food is involved in planning discussions involving agricultural land
- the Secretary of State for Energy on power stations.

However, it is the Secretary of State for the Environment (or Wales or Scotland) who has overall responsibility for framing and executing a national planning policy that is consistent and provides continuity. He can do this by making regulations, reviewing the structure plans of local planning authorities, intervening in local planning matters, deciding appeals, giving advice and laying down procedures. In controversial planning cases he can call in the application and decide it himself – especially where he feels that it is in the national interest to do so (for example, the siting of a major new settlement).

In practice the Secretary of State delegates most of his powers to Civil Servants, though he remains answerable to Parliament for the decisions taken in his name. In England the Planning Inspectorate deals with some aspects of the Secretary of State's work – see p. 66 for details. Regional offices of the Department of the Environment may also become involved in planning matters. In Scotland and Wales special departments of the Scottish and Welsh Offices deal with planning and development.

Apart from directly exercising his powers, the Secretary of State can influence local planning authorities in two ways: by binding regulations and by issuing advice and guidance. The regulations are made in the form of Statutory Instruments, which are laid before Parliament (usually passed on the nod). These cover matters such as developments which do not need planning permission, defining use classes and setting out the procedures for appeals. These Instruments are binding on local planning authorities – if they fail to follow them, their decisions can be overturned.

Advice and guidance is issued to local planning authorities through circulars from the Secretary of State, Planning Policy Guidance (PPG) notes, Mineral Policy Guidance (MPG) notes, handbooks and statements and parliamentary answers in the House of Commons. Policy statements are often made in this way – for example, on development proposals in the Green Belts or the government's approach to large shopping centres. A statement of policy by the Secretary of State is a 'material consideration' to be taken into account in making planning decisions, even by the Secretary of State himself. This does not mean that the statement is mandatory, but that what it says must be considered and only overridden for good reason. Circulars and Planning Policy Guidance notes are usually available to the public through HMSO bookshops (see p. 196), and can be helpful in preparing appeals or fighting development proposals.

Local planning authorities

Most planning decisions are made not at central government level but by the 'local planning authority'. The local planning authority depends on where you live:

- in the 47 'shire counties' of England and Wales there are two tiers of local planning authority, the county and district councils. The planning function is shared between them, though for most day-to-day contact you deal with the district council

- in the Greater London area and the six metropolitan counties (Greater Manchester, Merseyside, South Yorkshire, Tyne & Wear, West Midlands and West Yorkshire) there is only one tier of local government, the district councils and London boroughs – these are the only local planning authorities in these areas
- in Scotland it is the district councils where these exist, and the regional or island councils elsewhere.

Where there are two tiers of local planning authority, the higher authority (county or region) is responsible for overall strategic planning in its area. It also has specific responsibilities for roads, waste disposal and mining. The lower authority (the district) takes care of detailed planning down to site level, including administering the planning permission system. Where there is only one local planning authority, all these functions are concentrated on it.

In some cases (for example, National Parks) the Secretary of State imposes special arrangements by creating a joint board that takes on the role of a county council or district council. And there are special planning areas which the Secretary of State can set up, such as urban development corporations and enterprise zones – see p. 165.

There is no regional tier of government in England and Wales which can co-ordinate planning and development across county boundaries. But there are regional planning organisations in several parts of the country which fulfil this function. For example, the planning authorities for London and the south-east meet in SERPLAN, the South-East Regional Planning Conference – and this acts as a forum to discuss regional issues between the members and with the Secretary of State. Other regions have similar organisations.

Local councils, the Crown and statutory undertakers

There are special planning rules for these three groups.

Local councils must apply to themselves for planning permission when they wish to develop land. After passing a resolution to seek the permission, they go through the same consultation processes as anyone else, before giving themselves the permission they need. There is no appeal against this decision.

Development by the Crown – that is, government departments – does not need planning permission. But the government has agreed that its departments should notify local planning authorities of their intentions. The plans will be publicised in the same way as applications from ordinary people, with the right to lodge objections. If the local planning authority objects to the plans (as it may do with a prison, say), the objections will be referred to the Secretary of State, who will deal with them as a normal appeal.

Statutory undertakers are organisations defined by the Town and Country Planning Act 1971 as providing certain services: railways, telecommunications, road transport, water transport, electricity, gas, water, sewerage and the like. Much of their routine work does not need planning permission – it is permitted development under the General Development Order (see p. 31). If they do need planning permission, they apply in the normal way to the local planning authority (unless the work already has the go-ahead of a government department – for example, for the compulsory purchase of land). With an appeal, the Secretary of State will consult the government department responsible for their work before making a decision (for example, for gas, with the Secretary of State for Energy).

The development plans

One of the most important tasks of the local planning authority is to build a framework of plans to cover its area. It does this in consultation with people living in the area, and the Secretary of State must approve the high-level structure plan. The making and reviewing of these plans offers an important opportunity to influence future planning priorities for the area you live in.

Where there are two local planning authorities, the county or regional council is responsible for a **structure plan** for the whole county or region (see below). The district council prepares the **local plan** (see p. 162) and administers the planning permission system. In metropolitan counties and Greater London, all the functions are carried out by the district council and a single **unitary development plan** (UDP) (see p. 163) is prepared.

The structure plan

The structure plan deals with the major planning issues for the area it covers: for example, the number of new homes required and the areas earmarked for them; the provision of education, community services and recreation; utilities; roads and transport; jobs and industry; shops and offices. The structure plan will set out the local planning authority's general policy for development in the area – what will be permitted, what will be encouraged and what will be discouraged, for example. It will include policies for developing the area – provision of new homes and amenities, improving the environment and managing traffic. And it may identify action areas selected for comprehensive development or redevelopment.

The structure plan takes the form of a statement summarising these policies and proposals, with diagrams and schematic maps to illustrate it. The table on p. 161 lists the contents of a typical structure plan. An explanatory memorandum summarises the reasons behind each policy decision in the plan. Special subject plans may deal with matters such as waste disposal, mineral extraction and the Green Belt.

In drawing up or amending its structure plan, the local planning authority has to take into account several factors:

- the plans of neighbouring areas
- national and regional policies (the latter may reflect strong guidance from the Secretary of State – see p. 161)
- the resources available (that is, the plan must be realistic)

POLICY SUBJECTS IN A TYPICAL STRUCTURE PLAN

Housing, including details of the number of new houses to be built and their distribution in each district

Industry and commerce, with land proposed for new developments

Shopping – the areas to be regarded as centres and those which are to provide local facilities

Settlement pattern, including which towns and villages are scheduled for expansion

Transport and communications, with proposals for improving traffic management

Agriculture and forestry – including conservation issues

Minerals – sites to be exploited and those to be restored

Waste disposal strategies, including pollution control

Environment – protection and conservation measures

Green Belts and their location

Recreation and tourism, including facilities and access

Social amenities – schools, hospitals, social services, etc.

- social policies and considerations – it is not enough just to go for the cheapest or most cost-effective proposals.

The Secretary of State influences structure plans by issuing policy statements and guidance notes. Since his approval for the plan is necessary, his advice cannot lightly be overlooked. For example, the government has identified various planning problems arising in the south-east of England, especially connected with changes in industry, housing demands and the consequences of the Channel Tunnel. And it has advised planners in the south-east to assume regional growth of over half a million homes between 1991 and 2001 – and suggested where these homes should be (see the table on p. 162).

Structure plans now cover the whole country, and as a rule are updated at five-year intervals.

WHERE NEW HOMES WILL BE NEEDED IN THE SOUTH-EAST, 1991–2001

Distribution of additional dwellings (inclusive of conversions)

Bedfordshire	20,000
Berkshire	29,500
Buckinghamshire	32,000
East Sussex	22,000
Essex	53,000
Hampshire	66,500
Hertfordshire	34,500
Isle of Wight	5,000
Kent	55,000
Oxfordshire	23,000
Surrey	26,000
West Sussex	28,000
SE counties total (rounded)	395,000
London	175,000
TOTAL	570,000

Source: *Regional Guidance for the South-East*, Department of the Environment PPG9 (February 1989)

The local plan

If the structure plan makes provision in your area for housing or whatever, the local plan will get down to street and even site level to spell out what these strategic targets mean locally. Local plans are drawn up within the framework decided by the county structure plans, with four aims:

- to develop the structure plan in more detail
- to provide a framework for considering planning applications

- to co-ordinate proposals for the use of land
- to highlight detailed planning issues for public discussion.

A local plan will normally cover an entire town or district, but more detailed plans still may be drawn up for action areas needing special attention. Separate subject plans may be drawn up to look at matters such as roads or recreation provisions. And local planning authorities often draw up development briefs for sites which are ripe for development (for example, disused industrial land); the brief usually gives positive encouragement for particular uses and plans.

The local plan consists of a scale map and a written statement with proposals for the area covered together with the arguments which led to those proposals. Extra diagrams and descriptions may be included, and the plan must include proposals to improve the environment and traffic management.

Ideally, local plans would cover the whole country, but at present only around a quarter of the country is covered by them. They usually relate to problem areas which are under pressure for development (such as villages in the south-east and in the Green Belt). But local planning authorities are encouraged to extend the coverage of local plans and many new ones are now in the pipeline.

The unitary development plan

Since the abolition of the Greater London Council and the six metropolitan county councils, there is only a single local planning authority in these seven urban areas. The 33 London boroughs and 36 metropolitan district councils fulfil this function, and they are responsible for drawing up single unitary development plans for their areas.

These come in two parts:

- Part i broadly covers the sort of issues in a county structure plan
- Part ii is the equivalent of the local plan.

The Department of the Environment has issued strategic guidance to reduce the chances of the various unitary plans clashing with each other.

How plans are produced

Structure plans require the approval of the Secretary of State after a lengthy consultation process with various bodies and the general public:

- district councils are consulted on their ideas, and they may in turn consult other bodies
- a draft structure plan is then produced. This is made available to the public and sent to official bodies, district councils and government departments for consultation (there is usually a six-week period for representations)
- the plan is finalised and submitted to the Secretary of State, who will accept it only if satisfied that the consultation process has been carried out properly
- at the same time, the plan is publicised and people who wish to make representations are invited to send them to the Secretary of State
- the Secretary of State then appoints a panel of experts (including a chairman) to carry out an examination in public of the key issues. This examination calls witnesses to give information and clarify the issues
- the resulting report is sent to the Secretary of State, who then approves the structure plan, rejects it or most commonly approves it with modifications (there will be a further period of consultation on any proposed modifications).

Local plans do not have to be submitted to the Secretary of State for approval (though he can call them in if he wishes). Instead, they are submitted by the district to the county or region which certifies them as conforming to the structure plan. Otherwise the procedure is similar, with a local public inquiry under an inspector who is appointed by the Secretary of State but who reports only to the district council.

Once plans have been produced, they must be updated from time to time, and fully revised when they become out of date. Most local planning authorities have a unit which monitors the plans and brings forward amendments.

Special planning areas

The system just described covers most of the UK. But there are a number of special planning areas, in both town and country, where the normal planning process might not produce the results desired.

New towns

Thirty-three new towns were designated between 1946 and 1970, largely to relocate people from cities such as London and Glasgow. Recognising that locally accountable councils were unlikely to welcome an inflow of population from the cities, it was decided that these new towns should be set up under the control and direction of central government. A development corporation was set up for each new town, with powers to acquire land and either develop it itself or arrange for private development. When the new town is finished, the development corporation is wound up and the area returns to normal planning procedures.

No new towns have been designated since 1970, though several are still in the development stage (including Telford, Milton Keynes, Cumbernauld and Cwmbran). If you live in a new town still under development, the development corporation is the local planning authority.

Urban development corporations

Since the end of the new town expansion, the emphasis has shifted to regeneration of inner-city areas suffering from industrial decay. The Secretary of State can create an urban development area in such inner-city locations, to remove some of the impediments to regeneration. The first two urban development areas were the London and Merseyside Docklands, and several others have now been created.

An urban development area is administered by an urban development corporation, the members of which are appointed by the Secretary of State. Their remit is to get things moving by attracting new industry and employment, clearing dereliction, providing housing and building infrastructure such as roads and rail links.

The corporation becomes the local planning authority and can ease new developments; more radically, the Secretary of State can sweep away restrictions on development which is in accordance with the development plan for the area. This means that it is harder to oppose development if you live in an urban development area.

Enterprise zones

Planning regulations can be relaxed in specific areas known as enterprise zones in order to help attract business and jobs. Enterprise zones offer all sorts of benefits to businesses, including cheap accommodation and no rates for ten years – and some freedom from planning red tape.

Enterprise zones can be set up only in areas that the Secretary of State thinks are suitable. He invites the local planning authority to propose an area and to decide what planning restrictions will be lifted – either naming specific projects or listing classes of projects that will not require planning permission.

Once an area is an enterprise zone, it may be impossible to oppose certain types of development. But since they will normally be set up in areas designated for industrial or commercial use, this may not directly affect residential areas.

Simplified planning zones

Local planning authorities can set up simplified planning zones (SPZ) in their areas where planning restrictions are relaxed for certain types of development. They don't need the say-so of the Secretary of State, though there is a public consultation procedure to follow. Anyone can propose setting up an SPZ – including developers; if the local planning authority turns a proposal down, there is a right of appeal to the Secretary of State.

An SPZ can be smaller than an enterprise zone, or even cover more than one site. The SPZ scheme will define the types of development that require no planning permission (together with any conditions), and once the scheme is adopted it lasts ten years. An SPZ cannot be set up in conservation areas, Green Belts, National Parks and Areas of Outstanding Natural Beauty.

Green Belts

Green Belts are areas of countryside around built-up areas. The normal planning procedures operate, but the government lists five special planning aims for the Green Belts:

- to check the sprawl of large towns and cities
- to safeguard the countryside around the towns from further building and urban sprawl
- to prevent neighbouring towns from merging
- to make sure that the character of historic towns isn't spoilt by overdevelopment
- to help regenerate towns and cities by stopping developers from just expanding into new territory.

Green Belts are set up with the approval of central government, but the exact boundaries are decided by the local planning authorities. It's not impossible to build on Green Belts, but it won't normally be allowed. Exceptions might include developments for recreation or agriculture.

There are 15 Green Belts in England, covering 4½ million

acres (one-seventh of the country), while in Scotland there are five. Their size varies from 2000 acres (around Burton-on-Trent) to over a million acres (around London). Not all of it is ‧ green and pleasant – it includes neglected and run-down areas, and most of it is not open to the public.

EXAMPLE: GREEN BELT BROWNED OFF

A new village of 900 houses is to be built in the London Green Belt near Shenley in Hertfordshire. It will occupy the site of a psychiatric hospital scheduled for closure as part of the move towards care in the community.

The developers plan to site the village in a rural park open to the public, and were able to argue that this improved the Green Belt amenities. The proposal went to a public inquiry, where opponents argued that it conflicted with guidelines issued by the Secretary of State for the use of Green Belt hospital sites (these suggest that either alternative uses be found for the existing buildings or replacement buildings be allowed only if they cover the same area). The inspector gave the application the benefit of the doubt, though this established no precedent for other such sites.

National Parks and AONBS

Stricter planning regulations apply in Britain's National Parks and Areas of Outstanding Natural Beauty (AONBS) – see p. 98 for more details. These are areas of countryside whose natural beauty is worth preserving. With National Parks, the local planning authority has a duty to promote the parks' enjoyment by the public. These controls are not intended to interfere with the economy and life of the area.

Sites of Special Scientific Interest

More than 4000 areas of land or water containing plants, animals, geological features or landforms of special interest have been designated Sites of Special Scientific Interest (SSSI) by the Nature Conservancy Council (NCC). Developments requiring planning permission on these sites is allowed only after consultation with the NCC

Once the NCC has decided to create a Site of Special Scientific Interest, it notifies the owners, the occupiers, the local planning authority, the Secretary of State and the water and drainage authorities. The notification includes a list of operations which would damage the special interest of the site. Owners and occupiers must write and tell the NCC before doing any of these operations, and the NCC will refuse permission if it thinks that the proposed operation will damage the site.

The NCC does not have to be told about operations if planning permission for them has already been obtained. However, the local planning authority is required to consult the NCC if considering a planning application regarding a Site of Special Scientific Interest – so it will speed things up if the NCC is informed in advance.

There are tax concessions to help the owners or occupiers of SSSIs. And the NCC has powers to help landowners manage SSSIs, including making grants and compensation payments. As a last resort the NCC will even lease or purchase the site – and can apply for a compulsory purchase order.

A booklet on Sites of Special Scientific Interest is available from the Nature Conservancy Council (address on p. 197).

Agricultural land

Local planning authorities preparing structure plans and unitary development plans are required to consult the Ministry of Agriculture, Fisheries and Food as part of the planning process. If the Ministry objects to proposals for agricultural land, it can ask the Secretary of State for the Environment (or Scotland or Wales) to call in local plans.

And planning applications that involve the loss of sizeable chunks of high-grade farmland must be referred to the Ministry by the local planning authority.

169

These provisions were introduced because of the importance of food production in the national economy. But as a member of the European Community, Britain is now seeking to reduce agricultural output as part of the drive to reduce surpluses and cut the cost of the Common Agricultural Policy. As a result, farmers are encouraged to take land out of production either to conserve it or to convert it to other uses, such as for recreation and sport.

Major planning projects

Earlier chapters have dealt with planning applications for small and medium-sized developments. But recent years have seen some gigantic development projects, such as whole new villages, major motorways, out-of-town shopping centres and industrial estates and even the rail link to the Channel Tunnel. The planning procedures for these large projects are essentially the same, but often turn out rather different from smaller applications.

For example, a large project by a private developer may involve a degree of partnership with the local planning authority to share benefits – so-called planning gain. Major public sector projects may be excluded from the planning system altogether, with parliamentary bills to give them the go-ahead.

Planning gain

Any developer applying for planning permission for a major development can end up negotiating with the local planning authority over conditions. For example, the developer may have to reduce the number of houses per acre, or landscape the surroundings or provide better access or parking facilities. An out-of-town shopping centre may get the go-ahead only if some small business workshop units are built as well. Increasingly in recent years, developers have gone beyond the details of the planning application to offer amenities which will be of benefit to the local community.

For example, the developer who succeeded in getting the go-ahead for redeveloping London's Spitalfields Market area reportedly promised a package of community benefits for the London Borough of Tower Hamlets, the local planning authority. Permission to build a housing estate on the fringe of a village might bring a new sports centre for the whole village, and so on.

These so-called planning gains arise because there is a shortage of suitable land for particular developments. The developer who can get permission for a patch of land may see its value shoot up so that land worth a few thousand pounds becomes worth millions. The planning gain redistributes some of that windfall to the community, often the only way that the community will currently benefit.

The problem with planning gain deals is that there can be a fine line between sharing benefits and buying planning permission – bribing the local planning authority. The Department of the Environment has recently warned against deals which bring facilities or benefits not directly related to the development in question. Examples of acceptable gains include:

- provision of community housing on private developments which can be allocated to housing associations to meet local needs
- including community facilities such as libraries and sports halls in retail developments
- creating jobs on the development for local people, if necessary with suitable training
- improving the infrastructure (roads, water, sewerage, etc.) where it would be under pressure from the development anyway.

For people working to conserve their environment, such planning gain deals can create a dilemma, because by opposing a development they may lose benefits for the whole community, which with the tight financial constraints on local government may not come from elsewhere. One yardstick would be to value the benefits to be gained by the community and compare them with the gains to be made by the developer. A useful guide to evaluating such deals, called *Planning Gain*, is available from Planning Aid for London (address on p. 198).

Major infrastructure developments

Where a planning application seems likely to be controversial, the Secretary of State can call it in to decide for himself. Invariably, this will lead to a public inquiry, as with the new village at Foxley Wood (see p. 178), the new coal-mine at the Vale of Belvoir in Nottinghamshire and the extension to Stansted Airport. In exceptional cases the planning system will be sidestepped completely by means of a special Act of Parliament, as happened for the Channel Tunnel and will probably happen for the rail link between the Channel Tunnel and London.

A public inquiry in these circumstances can be a protracted and costly affair – for both the developer and the opponents. The inquiry over Sizewell B, for example, lasted over two years, and was held in a remote part of Suffolk near the site. Opponents challenged every aspect of the plan, including the need for more generating capacity, the result for jobs, and issues of engineering safety, in addition to strictly planning criteria.

A Parliamentary Bill is quicker, though it must be scrutinised by a committee of MPs. And it is not just public sector projects that can bypass the planning system through Parliament: private developers can promote a Private Bill, as happened with the extension to Felixstowe Docks. Although this offers less opportunity for opponents to intervene directly, they can try to influence the MPs through the normal means of lobbying, petitions, etc. (see p. 186).

Finally, major road developments are outside the development planning system. The Department of Transport initiates motorway and trunk-road schemes, and must hold a public inquiry locally if there are objections. This works in much the same way as a local planning inquiry.

═ 10 ═

DEFENDING YOUR LOCAL ENVIRONMENT

This chapter looks at how you should approach a major planning development which threatens to change your area irrevocably for the worse. There are details of how to oppose the application and how to follow this through if the developer appeals. Some recent case studies are illustrated to show how they succeeded.

Much of the procedure is as already set out in earlier chapters. In particular, Chapter 7 explains how to object to a planning application and fight a developer's appeal. But with major planning battles, the scale of your campaign will need to be greater.

Never be a loner

The emphasis in Chapter 7 on joining forces with others cannot be emphasised too much with major developments. A lone objector has defeated developers before, but the odds are greatly strengthened if you are part of a community group. See p. 130 for tips on forming a group.

If you are part of a group already, look for allies among other groups also likely to be affected by the proposal. Major developments can affect several communities, but the effect is weaker if each community campaigns alone. Worse, opposing groups may be played off against each other – or you may succeed at the expense of another.

TIP

Don't be deterred from opposing a major development, no matter how much the odds seem to be stacked against you. There is no guarantee of success, but if you don't try you certainly won't succeed. Some apparently hopeless campaigns have led to victory (as the example of Foxley Wood on p. 178 shows – only a government reshuffle won the day). If you are unsuccessful, at least you will know you did everything possible – and you may win useful concessions.

Take a proactive approach

Once a planning application is lodged, time can seem very short for mobilising opposition, especially if it's several days before news of the application leaks out. You can give yourself more time – and perhaps head off possible applications – by taking a proactive approach, rather than just reacting to developers' applications.

For example, you can try to be put on the list to be notified of planning applications so that you hear about them quicker (the council is more likely to agree to this for a group than an individual). If you live in an area attractive to developers, you can organise obstacles to deter them:

- create amenities on waste land – nature reserves, leisure sites or playgrounds (see p. 143)
- get the council to chase up freeholders who are letting land or buildings fall derelict (see p. 143)
- have Tree Preservation Orders (TPOs) put on strategically placed landmark trees (see p. 151)
- make sure that buildings of historic or architectural interest are listed, especially if you think that a developer plans to demolish them (see p. 149)
- if you think that your area is of architectural or historic interest, ask the local planning authority to make it a conservation area (see p. 147).

If you see people wandering around with theodolites and surveying equipment, ask them why. It may be the council surveyor – or it could be a foray by a developer. If a developer has a choice about where to build, the site that elicits the least opposition is always preferable.

Get involved in planning for your area

The single most important way to influence the development of your area is through the structure and local plans (or the unitary development plan in a metropolitan area). When these are drawn up or revised, there is extensive consultation with local people – especially amenity groups. Once a plan is approved, it may be hard to argue against the types of development it proposes: on the other hand, having your area designated for the sort of development you prefer can effectively inoculate it against other types of development.

Use the consultation opportunities which the process of adopting a plan involves to influence the plan (see p. 164). With a structure plan, there will be the examination in public, which offers an important opportunity for local pressure groups to change the proposals of the local planning author-

---

COIN STREET'S ALTERNATIVE PLAN

Local residents of the Waterloo and north Southwark area spent ten years in the 1970s and early 1980s fighting proposals to redevelop Coin Street with high-rise hotels and offices. In 1984, with the help of the Greater London Council, the residents were able to buy the derelict 13-acre site through Coin Street Community Builders, a non-profit company, all of whose members are local residents. Their plans to develop the site include co-operative housing, shops, workshops, cafés, leisure facilities and a social centre – the sort of building that the big developers were unwilling to provide in such an inner-city area.

---

ity. You can also intervene when a local plan is drawn up: if there are objections to the proposals, there must be a local plan inquiry at which the objections can be aired.

If there isn't a local plan for your area, ask the local planning authority to prepare one (especially if there is pressure for development). This opens up a public discussion and you can even draw up your own plans for the area and put them forward. And make sure that you have won the support of your councillors for the ideas you are putting forward: even if they endorse them in the plan, it will need their efforts to make it a reality.

Mobilising against proposals

If you are sufficiently determined to resist a major development, the developer may decide not to waste time and effort and look for a site elsewhere. After all, a protracted battle may not only be costly, but could mean no permission at the end or permission on terms that make the project less profitable. But by the time you learn of the developer's interest, it will probably be past the point of no return, and you must then set up a plan of action to defeat the proposals.

Your plan should be pursued in three steps, assuming that the developer can't be dissuaded from going ahead:

Step 1: Campaign against planning permission being granted for the application If it is difficult for the local planning authority to refuse permission, then campaign for it to be granted only subject to strict conditions that protect the character of your area.

If it appears that the local planning authority is likely to grant permission, try to get the application called in by the Secretary of State. This will mean a public inquiry. Remember that if the developer gets acceptable planning permission at this stage, there is no further opportunity for objections to be heard.

Step 2: If there is to be an appeal, lobby for a public

inquiry A public inquiry allows objectors to put their case more forcefully than with a written appeal.

Step 3: Campaign for the appeal to be turned down by the inspector (or the Secretary of State) If the appeal is upheld, you have almost certainly lost the battle.

Where the Secretary of State calls in an application to decide it himself, this eliminates steps 1 and 2 – but makes the public inquiry and step 3 the only opportunity to win the case.

Strengthening your organisation

The campaign against a development needs a focal-point around which people can gather. This includes a central point for information, organisation and contacts, preferably with someone available at all times. As the case of Foxley Wood indicates (see p. 178), success may require the equivalent of an office with full-time staff.

The basic minimum is an address and a telephone number to provide the focal-point. You can base the campaign at someone's home (a separate room is highly desirable). Alternatively, a sympathiser may be able to lend a vacant office or shop for the period of the campaign, which is more central and avoids disrupting someone's home.

A telephone contact number is also essential. If you can possibly afford it, have a special line put in which isn't used for private purposes. The maximum cost of installation is just over £100, and the quarterly rental around £30 (there'll also be the call charges, of course). A cheap answering machine costs well under £100 and will ensure that messages can always be left. You can also put some basic campaign information on the tape that greets callers (for example, 'Coaches for the lobby of Parliament leave the village green at 7.30am on 12 October').

Access to typing or word processing facilities is also important. Letters will have to be written, documents drafted and submissions drawn up for official consideration. It ought to be possible to avoid buying equipment – supporters will have their own, and perhaps be prepared to lend them. If not, you may be able to hire a good electric typewriter locally. And spend a little money on printing some notepaper with an eye-catching letterhead – it may be the only thing that persuades recipients to read your letters.

Lastly, access to a good-quality photocopier will help in producing campaign materials and the necessary copies of documents and submissions. A local business may give you access at cost; alternatively, ask a local copy shop to give you a special deal in return for publicity.

The campaign centre also provides a place for the work of stuffing envelopes, folding inserts, and so on. If you can have it manned during normal office hours, evenings and week-ends, this will help in dealing with the tight timetable a planning campaign involves (and the volunteers on shift can always busy themselves with practical work).

EXAMPLE: STAVING OFF A NEW TOWN

Consortium Developments Limited, a group of ten major housebuilders, sought planning permission in 1986 to build a new country town of 4800 homes, to be called Foxley Wood. It would have occupied 800 acres of gravel workings, heath-land and plantation between Bramshill and Eversley on the Hampshire/Berkshire borders. Although the area was not earmarked for housing in the Hampshire structure plan, the county is expected to find 66,500 new homes by 2001 – and a new town offered the chance to meet a large part of that target.

Local residents vigorously opposed the plans, and launched a £30,000 campaign to save the area. Called Sane Planning in the South-East (SPISE), it saw its role as going beyond the Foxley Wood case to look at planning throughout the region (Consortium had plans for 14 other villages in the south-east).

The SPISE executive committee included at various times a solicitor, a planner, two bankers, councillors, scientists and others from the world of business, conservation and public affairs. Secretary Tony Fletcher gave up his full-time work, and lived on a small navy pension to put up to 18 hours a day into the campaign. Another committee member, Sue Archer, reckons it became a full-time occupation for her too: 'At one stage I was on the end of the telephone for 12 hours'.

Bramshill Parish Council donated money and helped organise sponsored walks and horse rides. Thousands of leaflets were distributed – through doors, on car windscreens and in the streets. The planning application was turned down by Hart District Council. But Consortium appealed and a public inquiry was launched, with the final decision to be taken by the Secretary of State, at that time Nicholas Ridley.

SPISE organised local people to give evidence at the inquiry, including doctors to point out the strain that Foxley Wood would put on medical services. They pointed out that the sewerage services could not cope, and commissioned transport consultants to analyse the impact on local roads. Thousands of pounds were spent on hiring experts, and 25 local people gave evidence.

Even after the end of the inquiry, SPISE kept up the pressure, with press releases, lobbying people in high places and attending national conferences. The inspector agreed with their case in his report, concluding that 'there are no conditions which could adequately correct the balance in favour of planning permission where the costs, particularly in terms of the harm to conservation interests, countryside and highways, outweigh the benefits, as in this case'. But the Secretary of State announced that he was 'minded' to uphold the appeal – this allowed a further period for submissions (see p. 84).

Local anger erupted with a furious rally at which an effigy of the Secretary of State was burnt. SPISE intensified its national campaign, bringing in local MP Julian Critchley. He tabled an Early Day Motion on the Secretary's intentions and mobilised sympathetic MPs in the south-east. In the end it was a government reshuffle that saved the day – a reshuffle that many commentators thought was occasioned by mounting national disquiet over 'green' issues.

The new Secretary of State, Chris Patten, appeared more responsive to conservation issues. Ever keen to maintain the pressure of publicity, SPISE still did not let up: written comments and 50 petitions were delivered to Mr Patten's office by Julian Critchley in a Victorian state coach pulled by two grey horses. The new Secretary upheld the inspector's report, as the idea of a new town was not envisaged in the Hampshire structure plan. SPISE remains in existence to advise other local groups in similar cases and to promote positive planning policies for the south-east.

Putting your case together

The key to success in opposing a development is the case you can put together: campaigning helps a good case to succeed (and may even assist a marginal case); no amount of campaigning can make a bad case stick.

Beware of being abusive in setting out your case. Your feelings about the developer may be less than charitable, but these feelings may not be shared by the people you want to influence, especially if the developer is promising some benefits for the community. The reasonableness of your case will convince – mindless abuse will alienate (and may be actionable).

Study the plans

The most important tools in putting together your case are the plans for the area – the structure plan and the local plan. It could be almost impossible to defeat an application to build houses on land earmarked for housing on both plans (provided the application fits in with other aspects of the plan, such as density of housing, materials, and so on). But an application for development that does not fit in with the plans for the area tends to throw the burden of proof on to the developer, who must demonstrate factors which override the plans.

So start putting your case together by looking at the structure plan for the area where the development is to be located. The general policies for the kind of development proposed is the first point to note, but the plan will include a wealth of other details that have to be taken into account, such as traffic management and access. If there is a local plan, this may specify a particular use for the land in question and will have further more detailed policies. You will be able to identify whether the development impinges on areas with special planning rules – conservation areas, Areas of Outstanding Natural Beauty, enterprise zones or special planning zones, for example.

Look at the planning application in detail

Apart from the detailed maps and plans, the application will normally include statements with larger developments, setting out the rationale for the project, special aspects the developers wish to highlight as plus-points and details of how the project will be implemented. There could be scope to challenge these statements. For example:

- if the application claims that there is a demand for the shops, offices, sheltered homes or whatever, you could seek to show that there was more than enough of such property in the area
- if the developers are offering benefits to compensate for the loss of amenities (in a Green Belt, say), you could argue that the amenities are irreplaceable, that alternative sites are available which would not mean loss of amenities, or that the compensating benefits are inadequate or not necessary for the area
- you might attack the choice of materials as being out of character with the surroundings, or the landscaping as inadequate, or the building to be out of place in the site.

Making the changes necessary to meet such criticisms could make the project unprofitable.

Survey the site

Even if the land is scheduled for this sort of development, and even if the developer's application is reasonable in most respects, it is still open to you to argue that this particular site is unsuitable. For example, the access by road might be quite inadequate (particularly if lorries will have to use the completed development); there might be some scientific reason for preserving the site (a rare flower is found there, say).

There is, in fact, considerable scope for research by opponents of developments to highlight facts that would count against a development. For example, looking at similar developments might show that estimates of traffic in the application are unreasonably low. A survey could show that there is a glut of small business premises in the area, many of them still vacant. You could prove that an amenity which would be lost with the development is enjoyed by hundreds or thousands of people a year. The developer will have money and staff to build up his case. The opponents have their own ingenuity and local knowledge and must find the time and effort to build up a counter case.

Environmental assessments

Applications for large planning projects increasingly come with an environmental assessment, which deals with the impact of the development on the environment of the area. This is now a requirement under a European Community Directive for certain types of development, in particular those involving hazardous materials (toxic chemicals, for example) or processes (refineries, for example).

An environmental assessment is normally required only for developments on a significant scale (though smaller-scale projects in sensitive locations may require one). For example, brewing, making dairy products, tanning and pig rearing are among the processes which the government has specified for inclusion. If you feel that the application you're fighting has severe environmental impact, you might press for an environmental assessment to be prepared by the applicant, and scrutinise it carefully if one is submitted.

There's a Circular from the Secretary of State (Department of the Environment 15/88, Welsh Office 23/88) which sets out the requirements for environmental assessments (see p. 196 for address of HMSO Books).

Publicity for your case

Once you have assembled your case, don't sit on it until the inquiry comes along. Make sure that it is disseminated and publicised:

- leaflet homes and workplaces affected by the development, suggesting what people who agree with you should do and which arguments to use
- produce information packs for councillors, MPs, the press and local radio setting out your findings and arguments
- print window posters, car flashes, stickers, badges and T-shirts to show the depth of opposition – a poster in every window always makes an impact.

Running a successful media campaign may be the key to success with a major case: not only will it increase the support for your cause, but it may influence those who are involved in the decision. So don't just confine yourself to the local press if you need to reach figures outside your area: aim for daily newspapers such as *The Times*, *The Independent* and *The Daily Telegraph* (and their Sunday sisters), as well as Sunday newspapers like *The Observer* and *Sunday Correspondent*. Specialist periodicals may be helpful: the *New Civil Engineer*, *Local Government Chronicle* and environmental magazines, for example. Regional radio and television programmes may be interested, and they can also feed into national news bulletins and programmes.

An imaginative press and publicity officer can do much to achieve a higher profile, if only by writing good press releases which are the bread and butter of many local newspapers.

Building up your campaign

A publicity campaign could increase your chances of success by influencing those who must make the planning decisions. But it will also add weight to your opposition by demonstrating the scale of opposition. And the more people you involve, the more likely you are to build a better case against the development.

If you haven't already done so, approach local environmental groups or local branches of national organisations like Friends of the Earth or the Council for the Protection of Rural England. If there's a parish council or community council, make sure that they are lined up on your side. Try to involve councillors and MPs (see below).

One good way of getting publicity is to associate celebrities with your cause. Start with celebrities who live in your area, but also approach those with local links or antecedents. With some causes you may be able to enrol celebrities with no immediate connection with the area, because they support conservation causes in general; botanist David Bellamy has been prominent in campaigns to protect the countryside; film producer David Puttnam is President of the Council for the Protection of Rural England. Using celebrities to write letters to the press, address meetings, be present at stunts, and so on, can improve the impact of your campaign – and if you're raising funds their presence should increase the takings.

For a major planning application, you will need to consider various means of publicising your case and winning support, including petitions, meetings, demonstrations, stunts and lobbies.

Public meetings

Public meetings should be considered, to win new supporters, demonstrate the strength of feelings on a planning
proposal or simply for publicity. Certainly at an early stage,
the developers should be invited to put their case – if only
because a concerted opposition might make them think
twice.

Meetings near the site are the obvious step, but you might
consider a meeting at the town hall or county hall which
could draw in more councillors, pressure groups and other
amenity groups protesting about the proposals. Wherever
the meeting is to be, invite councillors, members of the
planning committee, the District Planning Officer, the local
MPS and the media.

A meeting requires careful planning if it is to be a success:

- pick a hall which will be full or even a bit overfull rather
  than one which will be half-empty
- don't pick a night when there is strong competition from
  some other event (the AGM of the parish council, say)
- draw up a programme for the meeting to ensure that
  speakers don't speak for too long, that members of the
  audience can contribute their views and that the meeting
  ends well before the hall has to be emptied
- try to have a celebrity either speaking or chairing the
  meeting – it will improve attendance and publicity
- make the hall look attractive, with a speakers' table on a
  podium, some flowers, a few posters and a welcoming
  atmosphere
- arrange for a microphone if the hall is large.

If you can find a special meetings organiser to concentrate
on this event, it will probably go better.

Demonstrations and stunts

Some sort of demonstration can help draw attention to
proposed developments, both in the media and to other

people who live and work in the area. If you can attach it to the site in some way, this will help put your case over – for example, by linking hands around it, or using rights of way to cross it. Try to make the demonstration entertaining and eye-catching with a carnival atmosphere. Inform the police and appoint marshalls to ensure that the demonstration is orderly and sticks to the plan (disorderly or violent demonstrations usually lose support for causes).

Suitable stunts can also highlight your case: a sponsored walk along a threatened path (this also raises funds); a parachute drop into fields under threat; stage a balloon race from the site using specially printed balloons with your campaign message; record a song setting out your case; stage a playlet in shopping centres and workplaces. Again, try to create a spirit of enthusiasm (people never warm to gloomy faces), make sure you get permission for anything you do, and stay on the right side of the law.

Lobbying Parliament

Lobbying MPs at the Houses of Parliament has long been a way of getting support and publicity for causes. It is also a good way of bringing concern before Ministers, who can call in controversial planning applications to decide themselves and who may make the final decisions on many planning appeals. Lobbying is often linked with the handing in of petitions, which local MPs accept and present to Parliament. If local MPs are not sympathetic, any MP can do it. You can also lobby the House of Lords, especially if you can enrol peers with a local connection to help.

If you plan to lobby Parliament, discuss this with sympathetic MPs and peers. They will be able to suggest a good day, book rooms inside the Palace of Westminster for meetings, gain access to Ministers and opposition spokesmen and women and otherwise help your lobby along. With a large lobby you may also decide to organise a London demonstration and a protest meeting at a large central London hall. Invite speakers for and against your case, and if you have celebrity supporters, use them as speakers – the press and TV love a famous name.

A friendly MP can do much to raise the issue at national level. He or she can:

- put down Parliamentary questions to Ministers – this can uncover useful information for your case as well as highlight local concern
- write letters to Ministers – the response is likely to be better than if ordinary people write
- raise the matter in the House, through Early Day Motions, adjournment debates and Ten-minute Rule Bills.

Large organisations, including many developers, now employ professional lobbyists to ensure that their case is heard. Professional lobbyists will use their skills and experience to make sure that Ministers, opposition parties, top Civil Servants and other influential people appreciate what the developer is up to. You must make sure that where decisions will be taken at central government level, your case gets equal exposure. Your numbers and enthusiasm are on your side: with really large planning applications you may find it necessary to get professional advice about lobbying. The cost is high, but if local councils or regional organisations are backing your campaign, you may be able to afford it.

Going to an inquiry

If you have succeeded in preventing a development from getting planning permission, the developers may well appeal against the refusal, especially if the stakes are high. In many cases this will be dealt with by written representations (see p. 76 for the procedure). But in big cases there will almost certainly be a public inquiry, held by an inspector. And where the Secretary of State calls in a planning application, that too will mean a public inquiry. For details of the formal procedure, see p. 78.

Presenting your case

Written submissions make up the bulk of the evidence even at a public inquiry. The inspector will inevitably have begun to form ideas and opinions from reading the documents submitted before the inquiry, and it is vital to make a good impact with them.

In producing a submission:

- give as much detail as necessary without unduly padding it out – the inspector will have too much to read, and a clear and concise exposition of your case will give a favourable impression
- err on the side of caution and include arguments only if they will stand up to scrutiny
- type or word process the submission, using a 'house style' for sub-headings, headers (a line at the top of every sheet that identifies the group and the document), footers (page numbers and date) and so on
- number the paragraphs to make it easier to refer to documents, and give letters or numbers to annexes
- give references for facts, figures and quotations.

Make enough copies for the parties at the inquiry and to distribute to the press (with a press release to save journalists the time of having to read it).

TIP

Be highly self-critical of written submissions, and redraft to perfect them. Get other people to read them – your own errors and omissions are hard to detect. The aim should be not to lose any points in your case: if in doubt, leave it out.

Expert witnesses

Many planning inquiries hinge on matters of fact or interpretation. You may be able to add weight to your case by calling an expert witness who has specialist knowledge on the point you want to bring out.

For example, a road inquiry will consider the need for roads and projections of demand – a transport consultant may be able to disprove the case for more roads. Historians, architects, botanists, zoologists and scientists may all be able to back claims you want to make for the site – and sustain the case through heavy cross-examination. Often, they will appear for nothing, but you should offer expenses at the very least. If they need to be paid, then a daily rate is usual, perhaps up to an agreed maximum.

If you need a specialist witness and haven't yet got one, approach environmental and conservation groups for suggestions. Local higher and further education institutions may have the right person, and professional advisers may have a network of contacts.

Professional advocates usually rehearse their expert witnesses in advance, both to familiarise themselves with the case and to explore possible weaknesses. This is well worth trying if you are representing yourself. The credentials of expert witnesses may be challenged under cross-examination: make sure that your expert isn't thrown into diffidence by false modesty.

Professional representation

A public local inquiry operates very much like a tribunal or court of law, with the developer on one side, the local planning authority on the other and objectors on the sidelines. Formal procedures are used, with cross-examination of witnesses and, on occasions, sworn evidence. Many appeals have been defeated by ordinary objectors conducting their own cases (as with the Pratts Bottom case study described on p. 190). But there are occasions when professional representation will be preferable – if you can raise the money.

The developer, for example, will have a team of legal advisers and planning specialists, all of whom will use their professional skills to challenge witnesses, including objectors. If the developer has succeeded with other planning applications of a similar kind, he will be able to draw on a fund of experience to know what will impress the inspector. A lawyer to represent you can ensure that your side is presented in the best possible light, and that the developer is fully challenged.

The problem is the cost: a solicitor is unlikely to be much less than £100 a day and could be more. If you need a barrister, this will mean more fees – anything from £150 a day to £1500 a day or more for a QC. A lower-cost alternative may be to use a planning consultant who has experience of representing people at planning inquiries (the Royal Town Planning Institute publishes lists of consultant town planners for each region; address on p. 198). And if you can't afford a consultant planner, try the planning aid services which exist up and down the country (see p. 28).

If you are intending to put your own case, it might still be worth buying a few hours of legal advice and briefing. A lay person can quite easily master planning law, but an experienced eye might spot some angles you would miss. An alternative to control the costs of expert representation is to use a lawyer to open your case, cross-examine and sum up and to use unskilled labour for the rest of the proceedings.

EXAMPLE: PRESERVING PRATTS BOTTOM

Many local people objected when the Prudential applied in 1986 to build a shopping and leisure centre on Green Belt farmland near Orpington in Kent. Bromley Borough Council refused the application, but the Prudential appealed to the Secretary of State for the Environment.

The Orpington and District Amenity Society ran a strong opposition campaign. They raised money and interest by selling 'protest packs', which included window stickers and lapel badges. A march of 4000 protesters along footpaths through the farmland got national media coverage. Fifteen thousand people signed a petition. Altogether, 31 local associations and over 2500 individuals sent in objections to the inquiry.

At the inquiry the Prudential claimed the proposal was a justifiable exception to the Green Belt policy. It said that the community would benefit from the new facilities, and the Prudential would give a trust a large area of land accessible to the public. Bromley, supported by the local campaign organisations, argued that there weren't enough grounds to make the proposal an exception. The Orpington and District Amenity Society didn't hire lawyers: secretary John Alder presented evidence and cross-examined witnesses himself. 'Don't be overawed by the experts,' he advises.

The Secretary of State dismissed the appeal and made the Prudential pay Bromley's costs (estimated at £250,000). Although a large shopping centre in the Green Belt was unlikely to get an easy ride (the current government is firmly against them), local protesters still think the campaign was worthwhile: 'If we'd sat back and done nothing, the developers could have said no one really cares'.

Blight

Even if you are successful in your planning campaign, the threat of a major development can hang over your home for many years. It may become impossible to sell your property; if there is a buyer, the price will be much lower than before the threat materialised.

This so-called planning blight can be worse if you are not directly in the line of a development. Properties in the way of a road or major project will usually be compulsorily purchased (though the price may not fully reflect the value to you). If you are merely close to a development, there may be no compensation – even though the value of your home has plummetted. And until firm plans are published, it can be impossible to see from the vague sketching of the planner whether your home is affected or not.

Blight is most obvious with transport proposals – new roads and railways. The blight is often created as the result of road assessment reports, prepared for the Department of Transport by consultants. These may outline several broad options, affecting thousands of homes for months or even years – with no hope of compensation until definite plans are announced. But structure plans, new towns, urban development corporations and the decisions of statutory undertakers like local authorities or the utilities can all affect property-owners.

Once the plans are announced, the owner of a house on land that is to be used can then wait for compulsory purchase. You will normally get the market value of the house, plus disturbance compensation for reasonable expenses or losses created by the compulsory purchase (such as removal costs and legal costs). If you have lived in the property for five years or more, you can also get a small home loss payment to compensate for the upheaval. To get this you have to sit tight to the very end, maintaining the property to keep its value up. Alternatively, you may be able to serve a blight notice so that the house is taken off your hands straight away – with less by way of compensation.

TIP

If your area is threatened by a major development, the developing authority may have discretion to compulsorily purchase homes not directly affected. If you can't stop the development, a secondary objective of your campaign should be to ensure that the most favourable compensation package is negotiated. Pressure on councillors and MPs can help: British Rail has agreed to buy many more homes than are strictly necessary when it comes to building the Channel Tunnel rail link.

Blight notices

With a blight notice served on the developers you get the market value of the property plus expenses, but no home loss payment. If you own and live in a house on land which is in line for compulsory purchase (wholly or partly), you can serve a blight notice if you can show that you have made reasonable endeavours to sell the property but that you are unable to do so, or can do so only at a substantial loss. This means putting the home on the market with an estate agent.

The right to serve a blight notice doesn't apply to investment property (property you let out) or commercial property. And there are carefully specified circumstances in which you can claim blight; these include road plans, slum clearance and land which is required by the government. Most important for the private homeowner is that you can't serve a blight notice if your home isn't directly under threat of compulsory purchase.

So if the next-door house is to be flattened as part of a development scheme but yours isn't, you aren't eligible for blight compensation even though your home may be unsaleable. The only option under these circumstances is to seek compensation under the Land Compensation Act 1973 for the loss of value due to physical factors such as fumes, dust or noise. There's no compensation for the loss of amenity of living beside a motorway, privacy or view. In some circumstances you may be eligible for double-glazing grants. If your house is not offered this, you can appeal.

TIP

If your home looks as if it will be threatened by development, get it valued as soon as the plans are announced. Firm evidence of its market value may help in negotiating compensation. An estate agent may value the property for nothing. A surveyor will charge according to the level of work: £50 to £100 for a valuation, much more for a structural survey.

Free booklets on these types of compensation are published by the Department of the Environment and the Welsh Office (available from Citizens Advice Bureaux): *Your Home and Compulsory Purchase*, *Your Home and Nuisance from Public Development* and *Insulating against Traffic Noise*.

SOURCES OF HELP

Government organisations

England
Department of the Environment
2 Marsham Street, London SW1P 3EB
071-276 3000

Planning Inspectorate
Tollgate House, Houlton Street, Bristol BS2 9DJ
BRISTOL (0272) 218811

Wales
Welsh Office Planning Division
New Crown Building, Cathays Park, Cardiff CF1 3NQ
CARDIFF (0222) 825111

Scotland
Scottish Development Department
New St Andrews House, St James Centre, Edinburgh EH1 3SZ
031-556 8400

Northern Ireland
DoE (NI) Town and Country Planning Service
Commonwealth House, 35 Castle Street, Belfast BT1 1GU
BELFAST (0232) 321212

Planning Appeals Commission
Carlton House, Shaftesbury Square, Belfast BT2 7LB
BELFAST (0232) 244710

HMSO Books
St Crispins, Duke Street, Norwich NR3 1PD
NORWICH (0603) 694498
General telephone enquiries: 071-873 0011
Telephone orders: 071-873 9090

Ombudspeople

The Local Ombudsman
England
21 Queen Anne's Gate, London SW1H 9BU
071-222 5622
29 Castlegate, York YO1 1RN
YORK (0904) 630151

Northern Ireland
Office of the Northern Ireland Commissioner for Complaints,
33 Wellington Place, Belfast BT1 6HN
BELFAST (0232) 233821

Scotland
5 Shandwick Place, Edinburgh EH2 4RG
031-229 4472

Wales
Derwen House, Court Road, Bridgend, Mid Glamorgan CF31 1BN
BRIDGEND (0656) 661325

Parliamentary Ombudsman
Office of the Parliamentary Commissioner for Administration,
Church House, Great Smith Street, London SW1P 3BW
071-276 2130

Office of the Northern Ireland Parliamentary Commissioner,
33 Wellington Place, Belfast BT1 6HN
BELFAST (0232) 233821

Council on Tribunals
22 Kingsway, London WC2B 6LE
071-936 7045

20 Walker Street, Edinburgh EH3 7HR
031-220 1236

Official and advisory bodies

Cadw Welsh Historic Monuments
Brunel House, 2 Fitzalan Road, Cardiff CF2 1UY
CARDIFF (0222) 465511

Countryside Commission
John Dower House, Crescent Place, Cheltenham,
Gloucestershire GL50 3RA
CHELTENHAM (0242) 521381

Wales: Ladywell House, Newtown, Powys SY16 1RD
NEWTOWN (0686) 626799

Countryside Commission for Scotland
Battleby, Redgorton, Perth PH1 3EW
PERTH (0738) 27921

English Heritage (Historic Buildings and Monuments Commission)
Fortress House, 23 Savile Row, London W1X 2HE
071-734 6010

National Rivers Authority
30–34 Albert Embankment, London SE1 7TL
071-820 0101

Nature Conservancy Council (NCC)
Northminster House, Peterborough, Cambridgeshire PE1 1UA
PETERBOROUGH (0733) 40345

Royal Fine Art Commission
7 St James's Square, London SW1Y 4JU
071-839 6537

Rural Development Commission
141 Castle Street, Salisbury, Wiltshire SP1 3TP
SALISBURY (0722) 336255

Scottish Historic Buildings and Monuments Directorate
20 Brandon Street, Edinburgh EH3 5RA
031-244 3144

Planning bodies

Planning Aid for London
100 Minories, London EC3N 1JY
071-702 0051
*Free, independent planning service for community groups, residents'
associations and individuals unable to afford a consultant*

Royal Institute of British Architects (RIBA)
66 Portland Place, London W1N 4AD
071-580 5533
*The Community Architecture Resource Centre can help community and
voluntary groups with feasibility studies*

Royal Town Planning Institute (RTPI)
26 Portland Place, London W1N 4BE
071-636 9107
*A professional body for chartered town planners. The institute publishes
useful leaflets and lists of consultants in your region; local branches may
have volunteer services*

Sane Planning in the South East (SPISE)
Polbathic, Farley Hill, Reading, Berkshire RG7 1XE
ARBORFIELD CROSS (0734) 760439
*Campaigns against inappropriate development and for sensible planning
in the south-east*

Town and Country Planning Association (TCPA)
17 Carlton House Terrace, London SW1Y 5AS
071-930 8903
*Provides advice and information on planning and environmental matters
and access to professional advice*

Buildings conservation

Ancient Monuments Society
St Andrew-by-the-Wardrobe, Queen Victoria Street,
London EC4V 5DE
071-236 3934

Architectural Heritage Fund
17 Carlton House Terrace, London SW1Y 5AW
071-925 0199

Architectural Heritage Society of Scotland
43B Manor Place, Edinburgh EH3 7EB
031-225 9724

Civic Trust
17 Carlton House Terrace, London SW1Y 5AW
071-930 0914

Civic Trust for Wales
4th Floor, Empire House, Mount Stuart Square, Cardiff CF1 6DN
CARDIFF (0222) 484606

Council for British Archaeology
112 Kennington Road, London SE11 6RE
071-582 0494

The Georgian Group
37 Spital Square, London E1 6DY
071-377 1722

North-East Civic Trust
MEA House, Ellison Place, Newcastle upon Tyne NE1 8XS
091-232 9279

SAVE Britain's Heritage
68 Battersea High Street, London SW11 3HX
071-228 3336

Scottish Civic Trust
24 George Square, Glasgow G2 1EF
041-221 1466

Scottish Historic Buildings Trust
Saltcoats, Gullane, East Lothian EH31 2AG
GULLANE (0620) 842757

The Society for the Protection of Ancient Buildings
37 Spital Square, London E1 6DY
071-377 1644

The Victorian Society
1 Priory Gardens, Bedford Park, London W4 1TT
081-994 1019

Countryside conservation

Association for the Protection of Rural Scotland
14A Napier Road, Edinburgh EH10 5AY
031-229 1081

Council for the Protection of Rural England
Warwick House, 25–27 Buckingham Palace Road,
London SW1W 0PP
071-976 6433

Council for the Protection of Rural Wales
Ty Gwyn, 31 High Street, Welshpool, Powys SY21 7JP
WELSHPOOL (0938) 552525

National Trust
(England, Wales and Northern Ireland)
36 Queen Anne's Gate, London SW1H 9AS
071-222 9251

National Trust for Scotland
5 Charlotte Square, Edinburgh EH2 4DU
031-226 5922

Open Spaces Society
25A Bell Street, Henley-on-Thames, Oxfordshire RG9 2BA
HENLEY-ON-THAMES (0491) 573535

Ramblers' Association
1–5 Wandsworth Road, London SW8 2XX
071-582 6878

Royal Society for Nature Conservation
The Green, Witham Park, Lincoln LN5 7JR
LINCOLN (0522) 544400

Royal Society for the Protection of Birds
The Lodge, Sandy, Bedfordshire SG19 2DL
SANDY (0767) 680551

Scottish Wildlife Trust
25 Johnston Terrace, Edinburgh EH1 2NH
031-226 4602

Environmental groups and organisations

Airfields Environment Federation
West Wing, 5–11 Lavington Street, London SE1 0NZ
071-928 4933

Environment Council
80 York Way, London N1 9AG
071-278 4736

Friends of the Earth
26–28 Underwood Street, London N1 7JQ
071-490 1555

Greenpeace
30 Islington Green, London N1 8XE
071-354 5100

Shell Better Britain Campaign
Red House, Hill Lane, Great Barr, Birmingham B43 6LZ
021-358 0744

Tidy Britain Group
The Pier, Wigan, Greater Manchester WN3 4EX
WIGAN (0942) 824620

Transport 2000
Walkden House, 10 Melton Street, London NW1 2EJ
071-388 8386

UK 2000
PO Box 2000, London N1

Woodland Trust
Autumn Park, Dysart Road, Grantham, Lincolnshire NG31 6LL
GRANTHAM (0476) 74297

World Wide Fund for Nature UK
Panda House, Weyside Park, Godalming, Surrey GU7 1XR
GUILDFORD (0483) 426444

Community action

Common Ground
45 Shelton Street, London WC2H 9HJ
071-379 3109

Community Development Foundation
60 Highbury Grove, London N5 2AG
071-226 5375

Groundwork Foundation
Bennetts Court, 6 Bennetts Hill, Birmingham B2 5ST
021-236 8565

National Council for Voluntary Organisations
26 Bedford Square, London WC1B 3HU
071-636 4066

National Federation of Community Organisations
8–9 Upper Street, London N1 0PQ
071-226 0189

Northern Ireland Council for Voluntary Action
127 Ormeau Road, Belfast BT7 1SH
BELFAST (0232) 321224

Northern Ireland Voluntary Trust
22 Mount Charles, Belfast BT7 1NZ
BELFAST (0232) 245927

*Scottish Council for Community and
Voluntary Organisations*
18–19 Claremont Crescent, Edinburgh EH7 4QD
031-556 3882

Wales Council for Voluntary Action
Llys Ifor, Crescent Road, Caerphilly, Mid Glamorgan CF8 1XL
CAERPHILLY (0222) 869224

Further reading

See p. 206 for addresses of specialist publishers. Books out of print may be available through public libraries

Guides to planning law and processes

Effective Planning Appeals, Hilaire McCoubrey, BSP Professional Books, 1988

Encyclopedia of Planning Law and Procedure, Desmond Heap, Sweet & Maxwell. A four-volume looseleaf work with quarterly updates (hence the cost of £350 plus £175 a year – consult at a library): Volume 1, legislation up to 1969 (largely redundant); Volume 2, legislation since 1969; Volume 3, Rules and Orders; Volume 4, circulars and other publications from the Secretary of State

Enforcement – how unauthorised works and changes of use are dealt with through the planning system, Michael Clark, Planning Aid for London (address on p. 198), 1989

Listed Buildings, Roger Suddards, Sweet & Maxwell, 1988

Planning Appeals, Sweet & Maxwell. A bi-monthly magazine with extracts from recent appeals – consult at a library

Planning Applications and Appeals, Charles Mynors, Architectural Press, 1987

Planning Gain and Planning Agreements, Chris Marsh, Planning Aid for London (address on p. 198), 1989

Planning Law and Procedure, Michael Purdue, Eric Young and Jeremy Rowan-Robinson, Butterworths, 1989

Playing the Public Inquiry Game – an Objector's Guide, Wendy Le-Las, Viridis, 1989 (including addendum)

Scottish Planning Law and Procedure, Eric Young and Jeremy Rowan-Robinson, T. & T. Clark, 1985

Conservation

Amenity in Action, Civic Trust, 1989

Directory of Environmental Abbreviations, Edward Dawson, The Environment Council, 1988

Environmental Directory, Civic Trust, 1988

Environmental Grants, Susan Forrester, Directory of Social Change, 1989

Holding Your Ground – an action guide to local conservation, Angela King and Sue Clifford, Wildwood House, 1988

How Green is Your City – pioneering approaches to environmental action, Joan Davidson, Bedford Square Press, 1988

How to rescue a ruin by setting up a local buildings preservation trust, Hilary Weir, Architectural Heritage Fund

Information Guide Pack, Civic Trust. How to set up an amenity society

Regeneration – New Forms of Community Partnership, Civic Trust, 1989

Who's Who in the Environment: England, Sarah Cowell, The Environment Council, 1990

Who's Who in the Environment: Scotland, Sarah Cowell, The Environment Council, 1989

Organisation

A Guide to the Benefits of Charitable Status, Michael Norton, Directory of Social Change, 1988

Citizen Action – taking action in your community, Des Wilson, Longman, 1986

How to Run a Pressure Group, Christopher Hall, Dent

Organising Things – a guide to successful political action, Sue Ward, Pluto Press, 1984

People Power – Community and Work Groups in Action, Tony Gibson, Pelican, 1979

Seeing it Through – how to be effective on a committee, Steve Clark, Bedford Square Press, 1989

Starting and Running a Voluntary Group, Sally Capper, Judith Unell and Anne Weyman, Bedford Square Press, 1989

Using the Media, Denis MacShane, Pluto Press, 1983

Voluntary Organisations and the Media, Maggie Jones, Bedford Square Press, 1984

Fund-raising

A Guide to Company Giving, Michael Norton, Directory of Social Change, 1989

A Guide to the Major Trusts, Luke Fitzherbert and Michael Eastwood, Directory of Social Change, 1989

Charities Digest, Family Welfare Association, 1990

Directory of Grant-Making Trusts, Charities Aid Foundation, 1989 (and every two years)

Government Grants – a guide for voluntary organisations, Maggie Jones, Bedford Square Press, 1989

Funds for Your Project – a practical guide for community groups and voluntary organisations in Scotland, Scottish Council for Community and Voluntary Organisations (see p. 202 for address), 1988

Money and Influence in Europe, Edward Dawson and Michael Norton, VMG/Directory of Social Change, 1983

Please Give Generously – a guide to fund-raising, Anthony Swainson and Linda Zeff, David & Charles, 1987

Raising Money from Industry, Michael Norton, Directory of Social Change, 1989

Raising Money from Trusts, Michael Norton, Directory of Social Change, 1989

Researching Local Charities, Nancy Eaglesham, Directory of Social Change, 1988

The Complete Guide to Fund-Raising, P. W. and P. F. Sterrett, Mercury Books, 1988

Specialist publishers

Bedford Square Press
26 Bedford Square, London WC1B 3HU
071-636 4066

Charities Aid Foundation
48 Pembury Road, Tonbridge, Kent TN9 2JD
TONBRIDGE (0732) 771333

Directory of Social Change
Radius Works, Back Lane, London NW3 1HL
071-435 8171

Family Welfare Association
501 Kingsland Road, London E8 4AU
071-254 6251

Pluto Press
345 Archway Road, London N6 5AA
081-348 2724

Viridis
11 Roper Avenue, Leeds, West Yorkshire LS8 1LG